YORKSHIRE DALES
NATIONAL PARK

YORKSHIRE DALES
NATIONAL PARK

Tony Waltham

Webb & Bower
MICHAEL JOSEPH

Acknowledgements

This book was only made possible by the willing and constructive support received during its compilation from so many of the staff in the Yorkshire Dales National Park offices, but most of all to Chris Wood, the enthusiastic Information Officer. Sarah Priest and Alan King were two among many others who made positive contributions. To all these, due thanks, and also to the friends and colleagues with whom I've worked in the park, to the villagers and farmers I have met in the Dales, to my wife, and finally to Pete Gregory who first made me realize how special are the Yorkshire Dales.

Many of the photographs were taken by Tony Waltham. Other photographs were supplied by the following: Howard Beck 70; Charles Meecham 16, 18, 23, 24, 31, 43, 51, 104, 105, 116; Tom Parker 28, 30, 49, 55, 83, 89, 102, 111, 121; Simon Warner 95, 97, 112; Geoffrey Wright 62, 64, 78, 92; and the Yorkshire Dales National Park 42, 45, 77, 80, 87, 93, 94, 101, 106, 110, 114.

First published in Great Britain 1987 by
Webb & Bower (Publishers) Limited
9 Colleton Crescent, Exeter, Devon EX2 4BY
in association with Michael Joseph Limited
27 Wright's Lane, London W8 5SL
and The Countryside Commission,
John Dower House, Crescent Place,
Cheltenham, Glos GL50 3RA

Designed by Ron Pickless

Production by Nick Facer/Rob Kendrew

Illustrations by Rosamund Gendle/Ralph Stobart

Text and new photographs Copyright © The Countryside Commission
Illustrations Copyright © Webb & Bower (Publishers) Ltd

British Library Cataloguing in Publication Data
Waltham, Tony
The National Parks of Britain: the
Yorkshire Dales
1.   Yorkshire Dales National Park (England)
—Guide-books
I.   Title
914.2′04858   DA670.Y6.

ISBN 0–86350–138–9

Typeset in Great Britain by Keyspools Ltd., Golborne, Lancs.

Printed and bound in Hong Kong by Mandarin Offset.

Contents

Preface

The Yorkshire Dales is one of ten national parks which were established in the 1950s. These largely upland and coastal areas represent the finest landscapes in England and Wales and present us all with opportunities to savour breathtaking scenery, to take part in invigorating outdoor activities, to experience rural community life, and most importantly, to relax in peaceful surroundings.

The designation of national parks is the product of those who had the vision, more than fifty years ago, to see that ways were found to ensure that the best of our countryside should be recognized and protected, that the way of life therein should be sustained, and that public access for open-air recreation should be encouraged.

As the government planned Britain's post-war reconstruction, John Dower, architect, rambler and national park enthusiast, was asked to report on how the national park ideal adopted in other countries could work for England and Wales. An important consideration was the ownership of land within the parks. Unlike other countries where large tracts of land are in public ownership, and thus national parks can be owned by the nation, here in Britain most of the land within the national parks was, and still is, privately owned. John Dower's report was published in 1945 and its recommendations accepted. Two years later another report drafted by a committee chaired by Sir Arthur Hobhouse proposed an administrative system for the parks, and this was embodied in the National Parks and Access to the Countryside Act 1949.

This Act set up the National Parks Commission to designate national parks and advise on their administration. In 1968 the National Parks Commission became the Countryside Commission but we continue to have national responsibility for our national parks which are administered by local government, either through committees of the county councils or independent planning boards.

This guide to the landscape, settlements and natural history of the Yorkshire Dales National Park is one of a series on all ten parks. As well as helping the visitor appreciate the park and its attractions, the guides outline the achievements of and pressures facing the national park authorities today.

Our national parks are a vital asset, and we all have a duty to care for and conserve them. Learning about the parks and their value to us all is a crucial step in creating more awareness of the importance of the national parks so that each of us can play our part in seeing that they are protected for all to enjoy.

Sir Derek Barber
Chairman
Countryside Commission

Introduction

The Yorkshire Dales is a special landscape, matured from a unique blend of handiwork by both nature and mankind. Within the 680 square miles of the national park, there is a magnificent spread of wild moorland and pastoral valley, whose beauty and strength lie in the infinite variety of colour, texture and purpose. These contrasts distinguish the park landscapes, yet they are linked together by the threads of character which give the Dales an undeniable sense of unity and weld them into a single magnificent park.

The variety . . . is in the ground. The rock skeleton of the Dales shows its teeth in the dramatic limestone scars across the southern half of the park. Ingleborough and Malham lay claim to the finest limestone landscapes in Britain, with exposed rock pavements lying above an endless network of

Halton Gill, Littondale.

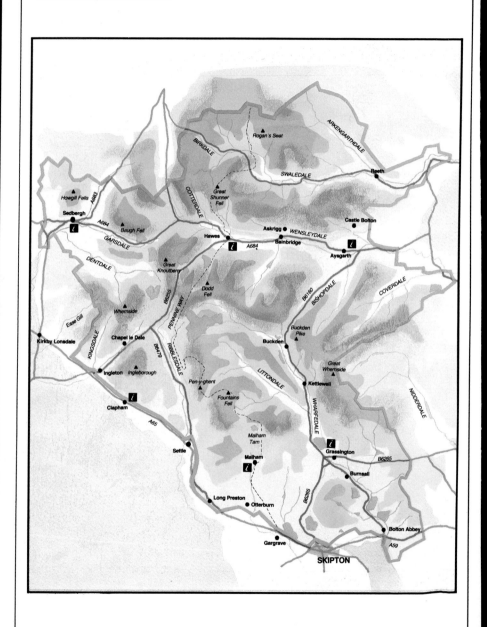

hidden caves. While further north, Swaledale winds between wild moorlands of gritstone, and the Howgill Fells have been moulded in ancient slate.

The variety ... is between man and nature. Ice Age glaciers fashioned the dales, scoured their broad, level floors and trimmed the fringeing scars such as Kilnsey Crag. But it was man who dressed the landscape with two thousand years of farming to clear the ancient forest and nurture the mosaic of meadow, pasture and open fell. And then for garnish he added the villages of stone, and achieved a perfect harmony where a tiny hamlet like Halton Gill nestles deep into the toe of a massive fell.

The variety ... is in the history. Reminders of bygone events arise in nearly every corner of the park. Early cave dwellers were followed by farming communities who left their ceremonial henge in Wensleydale, and then the Romans built their fort at Bainbridge. Ancient settlements and field terraces litter the flanks of Wharfedale, and just up the fell, Grassington Moor is fretted by the relics of the lead miners who came and went in the last few centuries.

The variety ... is through the seasons. Winter can last six months, when the plants don't grow, the sheep seem to survive the hardest of conditions, and the occasional combination of sun and snow turns the Three Peaks into an arctic wonderland. Then summer is a medley of warm pasture, rich hay meadow and sleepy village green, and the high fells are kind to their visitors. Even within the seasons there is variety: spring lambs may gambol on the dale floor while snow still hangs to the moorland horizons.

The variety ... is in the colour. Brilliant green pasture after a summer shower, and the yellow sea of June buttercups in the Swaledale meadow. Stark white of the limestone pavement contrasts with sombre dark of the gritstone edges. The northern moors are purple with heather, and Malham Tarn turns brilliant blue under a clear summer sky. Autumn brings fiery oranges to the woods of Wharfedale, and is followed by the black and white of shadowed fell walls across a blanket of new snow.

The variety ... is the landscape itself. The high open fell looks down on the deep secluded dale. The sound of silence can be heavy on the lonely moor, or it can be lost in the drone of the wind, while the dale woodland can be a haven of peace except where noisy water cascades on to rock. Sheep,

Facing The Yorkshire Dales National Park.

The limestone cliff of Kilnsey Crag rises sheer above the floor of Wharfedale, and looks across the river to the stone houses in the village of Conistone.

grouse and curlew can have the moors almost to themselves, but down below the old stone farmhouse is crowded into a patchwork of meadows.

Perhaps there, from farm to fell, is the symbolic thread which ties the Dales landscapes into one. The drystone walls lace almost every panorama in the park, and are a tangible link stretching from the dale floors high on to the moors and right over the towering summit of Pen-y-ghent. They epitomize the blend between man and the landscape, which has reached a splendid visual harmony in the dramatic hills and the picturesque villages. The Yorkshire Dales were born from natural erosion and grew up with the farmers; since 1954 they have made a spectacular national park.

1 **Rocks and scenery**

Landscape is carved by rivers and glaciers; but it is made by the rocks. Through almost any sequence of erosion, the hallmark of the rocks remains in the landscape which is eventually moulded. Different rock types create their own distinctive landscape styles, and none is more conspicuous in its scenic influence than limestone.

The Yorkshire Dales has an extensive limestone outcrop, and the national park was created to encompass its spectacular landscapes. But there are also other rocks which provide splendid contrasts and create a geological diversity in the scenery of the park. The major features of the park geology are delightfully simple, with a succession of rocks forming an almost level, layer-cake structure. In detail the rocks provide a fascinating story of ancient coral seas and invading deltas, but in terms of their influence on the landscape they fall into four broad groups.

Most of the rocks of the Yorkshire Dales are of Carboniferous age. This means that they were formed around 300 million years ago; they take their name because they contain most of the world's coal reserves, though there are only a few thin coal seams within the Dales. The limestone is the lowest unit in the Carboniferous of the park, and is overlain

Bare white rock identifies the landscape of limestone with its scars, crags and pavements on the fells above Malham.

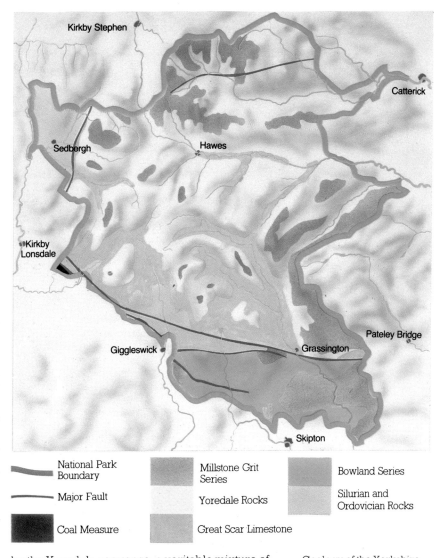

National Park Boundary

Major Fault

Coal Measure

Millstone Grit Series

Yoredale Rocks

Great Scar Limestone

Bowland Series

Silurian and Ordovician Rocks

by the Yoredale sequence, a veritable mixture of sedimentary rocks Highest of all in the geological succession are the Millstone Grits, which sit on top of the Yoredales. The fourth rock type of the park is a much more complex group of rocks, older than the Carboniferous and forming a basement to the area. The natural sequence for a geological study normally opens with the oldest rocks, but in this case it is best to leave the basement complex till later, and start with the limestone which dominates

Geology of the Yorkshire Dales.

the geology of the Yorkshire Dales.

It is impossible to miss the limestone in the southern half of the park. The white limestone cliffs characterize the park landscapes – whether they form the long terraced scars flanking Chapel-le-Dale, or the high unbroken walls of Gordale Scar. And besides these, there are the expanses of limestone pavement, the caves and the dry gorges; they all combine to make the limestone landscape the most distinctive of any rock, and the Yorkshire Dales has the finest in Britain.

Within the park there is one massive bed of limestone; it is a single slab, about 800 feet thick, reaching from Wharfedale in the east, past Malham, to beyond the park boundary west of Ingleborough. It has long been known as the Great Scar Limestone, but this term has proved to be rather imprecise, relying on boundaries which could not easily be put together. So geologists, who are concerned with the accurate record of the geological evolution of the area, now refer to the limestone as an upper Malham Formation overlying a lower Kilnsey Formation. Both names are of course derived from prominent landscape features, Malham Cove and Kilnsey Crag, and the Formations are now precisely keyed to the Carboniferous time-scale.

All the Great Scar consists of strong, compact limestones, so strong that they are unfortunately much in demand as a source of quarry stone. They are mostly grey in colour, though they range from cream to nearly black; the white of the limestone crags is just a weathering feature where a thin surface patina develops on exposure to the rain and atmosphere. Though most of the rock is composed of broken shell debris from marine animals, recognizable fossils are not as common as the optimistic collector may wish. Some beds contain the washer-like fragments of crinoid stems, the large, curved shells of brachiopods or packed masses of coral, but much of the limestone is disappointingly featureless.

Bedding planes and thin shales break the limestone succession. They form the horizontal lines across Malham Cove, and separate the beds to form the terraces of Twisleton Scars, north of Ingleton. The stronger beds then form the great expanses of limestone pavement which are such a feature all round the Ingleborough benches and on many of the other plateaux. Cutting through the limestone are dense systems of vertical joints. These give the clean angular edges to the limestone scars, and also guide the patterns of straight fissures across the pavements. The fractures, developed in the limestone by its deformation through geological time, provided natural channel for fluids migrating from sources deep below, and in some areas these fluids deposited minerals in the limestone. This is the origin of the mineral fields of Grassington and Swaledale, whose mining history we will return to later.

Most of the limestone was actually formed in warm, shallow seas. Tropical lagoons occupied most of the park area in early Carboniferous times, but there was deeper open water to the south. Waves breaking on to the edge of the shelf lagoons created an ideal environment for marine animal growth. Along the surf line, corals, algae, brachiopods and many more organisms built a line of reefs, mounds and submarine hills, which were subsequently buried by shales and some weaker limestones when the environment was slightly changed. Some of these buried hills of strong reef limestone have now reappeared in the Dales landscape, as selective erosion has removed their weaker cover rocks. They are called reef knolls, and the finest form a splendid group just south of Grassington; the conical hills of Kail, Elbolton, Stebden and Butter Haw are just appearing from beneath the shales of Thorpe Fell. And at Malham, Wedber Brow and Cawden Hill are two more reef knolls clearly recognizable by their shape.

The clear lagoonal seas, in which the limestone formed in early Carboniferous times, eventually succumbed to sand and mud washed in by deltas growing out from a northern landmass. Sea depths and delta activity were influenced by periodic earth movements which promoted cyclic sedimentation; each cycle brought first clay and then sand from the advancing delta, before the sea fought back to return to lagoonal conditions and limestone deposition. These then are the Yoredale rocks, repeated shale, sandstone and limestone, with each rock perhaps 40 ft (12 m) thick, but adding up to over 1,000 ft (300 m).

The northern half of the national park is dominated by the Yoredales, notably the entire valley sides of Wensleydale – whose ancient name of Yoredale christened the rocks. The contrasts of weak shales, with strong sandstones and limestones, provide the stepped topography which is the trademark of these rocks, and the limestones cap the many waterfalls which are a feature of the

Joints in the strong bed of limestone at the top of Malham Cove create a bold pattern in a fine stretch of limestone pavement, and have been added to by rainwater-cut solution grooves draining into them.

Stebden Hill and Butter Haw Hill are two of the spectacular group of limestone reef knolls just east of Cracoe. Relics of the Carboniferous seas, they now lie almost in the shadow of the grits of Thorpe Fell.

northern dales. Yoredale rocks also form the summit plinths of the Three Peaks rising above their broad limestone benches. But that far south there is less sandstone, and limestones form the steps on the slopes, notably that conspicuous rib halfway up Pen-y-ghent. Some of the Yoredale limestones are also noted for being very fossiliferous. A few are packed with the segmented cylinders of crinoid stems, and others contain great banks of coral; in this respect they outshine the Great Scar limestone. In the northern dales, the Yoredale sandstones are more important, and include some beds strong enough to be locally known as grits, and others which split into thin beds and therefore make excellent flagstones.

When the Carboniferous delta finally extended itself into the seas of the Dales area, sand became the dominant sediment. This then formed the strong sandstones, or gritstones, known as Millstone Grit. These lie in a thick sequence of shales and sandstones, of which only the lowest units occur in the national park. The two main rock types largely alternate with each other, though there are also horizons of flagstone and conglomerate, the coarse rock with large white pebbles of quartz which is so prominent on the ledges over the River Wharfe through the Strid ravine.

The Millstone Grit underlies the bleak heather moors which are so typical of the Pennines outside the limestone areas. These are the terrains of Great Shunner Fell and Grassington Moor, the latter developed on a particularly thick grit of the same name. The moors are a formidable landscape, so much in contrast to the splendour and detail of the limestone country. But where deep valleys provide steeper slopes, the strong grits stand out from the weaker shales to create the edges; these are scars of bare rock, dark and sombre to keep the contrast with their limestone cousins. Embsay Moor and Thorpe Fell are fringed by edges, though most of the Millstone Grit country is outside the Dales National Park.

Taking its name from the Wensleydale village, the Askrigg Block is the main geological structure within the Yorkshire Pennines. It is a deep-seated block of rock which has been steadily uplifted over hundreds of millions of years; most of the Dales National Park now sits on top of it. Surrounded by deep water, it provided the shallow seas where the Great Scar limestones formed. Now it forms the upland core of the Pennines, largely surrounded by lowland.

A massive bed of Millstone Grit forms the steep broken edge on the moors south of Grassington.

Earth movements have lifted and tilted the Block, so that the rocks on it now dip gently to the north-east. Along the southern edge of the Askrigg Block, a clean break has been created by the trio of massive fractures known as the Craven Faults. Though almost stable today, the faults were active over millions of years, and the rocks to the south have been displaced thousands of feet down below their relatives on the Block.

West of Settle, the Craven Faults are easily traced in the landscape, where they form the straight southern edge of Ingleborough; the South Craven Fault forms Giggleswick Scar, a splendid faultline with limestone to the north and younger, weaker shales to the south. At Malham, the North Craven Fault is just south of the tarn, edging the slate inlier on which the lake sits; the Middle Craven Fault marks the edge of the limestone plateau into which Malham Cove and Gordale Scar have been eroded, just north of the village; and the South Craven Fault is lost in the low country near Gargrave.

The western edge of the Askrigg Block is also faulted. But here the fault displacement has been the other way round, and across the Dent Fault older rocks have been lifted from far below. These are some of the basement rocks which underlie all the Carboniferous succession.

West of the Dent Fault, the Howgill Fells, together with Middleton Fell south of Sedbergh, are geologically part of the Lake District. Their rocks are mostly of Silurian age, which makes them about a hundred million years older than the Carboniferous succession in the Dales; they are mainly slates and compact grits, and are metamorphosed and complexly folded. These pre-Carboniferous rocks form yet another distinctive landscape type. The Howgill Fells are unlike the rest of the national park; their rounded shoulders, long steep slopes and deep ravines create a wild upland with none of the benching or geological detail which are the characteristics of the Carboniferous country.

Similar ancient rocks form the whole basement of the Askrigg Block, but are only exposed in a few small inliers where the Carboniferous rocks have been completely eroded away in the valley floors.

The largest inlier is in the floor of Ribblesdale, and reaches round into Crummack Dale. The Silurian and Ordovician rocks are mudstones, siltstones and a very strong variety of grit known as greywacke. They are well folded, so that ridges of

The rolling grassland of the Howgill Fells.

the greywacke cross the floors of both dales, and are also picked out by the quarries which sometimes expose spectacular fold structures. Within this sequence are the thin bedded flagstones quarried at Helwith Bridge and so conspicuous in the local buildings. Just isolated to the east of the main inlier, an outcrop of impermeable slates supports the waters of Malham Tarn, serene in its surroundings of dry limestone country.

The second inlier is at Ingleton, extending into both Chapel-le-Dale and Kingsdale, where slates and greywackes feed quarries past and present. The rocks are best seen in the Ingleton glens, where the rivers of both dales cascade through alternating vertical bands of the two rocks; each greywacke forms a waterfall and the slates are scoured out to form the intervening basins. But the finest of all the falls is different again. At Thornton Force, Kingsdale Beck cascades over a lip of Carboniferous Limestone, and drops into a plunge pool cut in Ordovician slates. Halfway down the force, the boundary is clearly exposed, with horizontal limestone sitting unconformably on the eroded ends of the vertical slates. Along the ledge behind the cascade, boulders of slate and greywacke are

Thornton Force, near Ingleton. Kingsdale Beck cascades over a staircase of horizontal limestone slabs, and then drops clear into the plunge pool in the weaker underlying slate.

clearly seen in the lowest limestone bed – relics of the storm beach formed when the Askrigg Block sank beneath the Carboniferous sea. Thornton Force is one of the classic sites of British geology, visited by countless student groups; and it is one of the keys to the fascinating geological history which lies behind the landscapes of the Yorkshire Dales.

2 **Legacies of the Ice Ages**

No grass, no soil, no rock; nothing but snow and ice. That was the Yorkshire Dales in the last Ice Age, 20,000 years ago; and the glaciers stamped their mark on the landscape in the grand style.

Covering most of the last two million years of geological time, the Pleistocene period was characterized by worldwide climatic changes which included the times of cooling which caused the Ice Ages. Sometimes the Pleistocene is known as the Ice Age, in the singular, but there was a long sequence of climatic contrasts; the ice sheets advanced and retreated across northern Britain at least three times in the last half million years, to create distinct glacial stages, or Ice Ages, in the plural, all within the Pleistocene. Each glacial advance contributed to the landscape erosion, but also removed most of the evidence of what had happened before. So, in the

The broad profile of Chapel-le-Dale has the distinctive U-shape which clearly tells of its glacial history.

context of the modern landscape, the most important event was the last glaciation – that known as the Devensian. The climate started to cool down about 100,000 years ago, and the ice built up to a maximum around 20,000 years ago; then 7,000 years later it had practically all melted away.

During the Devensian Ice Age, a massive ice sheet extended down from Scotland, joined with ice from the Lake District centre, and covered the whole Dales region. Probably 1,000 feet of ice lay over even the highest summits now within the national park. The main valleys of the Yorkshire Dales were buried far beneath the ice; they had already been established by river erosion during the few million years previous to the Ice Ages. Wensleydale, Wharfedale and most of the other dales do predate the ice, but they were then a little smaller, not so deep, and with narrower floors which were a little more winding. Though the Pleistocene ice, in each of its advances, swamped and overran the landscape, its pattern of flow was dictated by the existing valleys and hills. Beneath the vast ice surface, the ice flowed fastest along the valleys, scouring, enlarging, deepening and straightening them. Then, as the ice sheet waned and the hills projected as bare rock, discrete glaciers continued to erode the valleys.

So the dales we see today are glaciated troughs. Less than half their depth may be due to ice excavation; but the glaciers gave them their broad 'U'-shaped profiles and their straight clean lines, and turned them into textbook examples of ice erosion.

Within the national park, most of the ice flow was from the north-west, fanning out to both east and south. The high ground of Baugh and Great Shunner Fells, exposed to snow-laden winds from the Atlantic, formed a zone of accumulation known as the Dales Ice Centre. Also the Lake District and Scottish ice was pushing in from this direction. So the valleys aligned from the Dales Centre took most of the ice flow, and now have the most obvious glaciated profiles. To the south-east Wharfedale and Littondale are splendid glaciated troughs which rejoined their ice flows at Kilnsey.

The smaller details of the landscape, which provide the contrasts between the dales, also owe much to the ice. Limestone pavements on the Ingleborough plateaux and bare rock scars along many dale sides belong in the context of the karst landscapes (to which we will return in the next chapter), but both owe their origin to the scouring and plucking action of powerful ice flows. On a larger scale, glaciers could cut the ends off spurs as they straightened out the more devious river-cut valleys. Kilnsey Crag, and Arnberg Scar just a few miles further up the same valley, are both fine truncated spurs left with vertical and overhanging walls by the Littondale glacier.

But the ice cannot overcome all obstacles. Buckden Pike was high enough to deflect the ice which came down Langstrothdale from the west; some went down Wharfedale and some of the flow went over and into Bishopdale. Sheltered in the ice of Buckden Pike, the Walden valley was overrun by ice but was never scoured by any powerful flow; contrast its fluvial 'V'-shape with the glacial 'U'-shape of its Bishopdale neighbour.

Though the limestone areas of the Dales bear the widespread hallmark of ice action, the Howgill Fells present a different face. During the main Ice Ages, Lake District ice completely overran the Howgills, and because they stood so high, the ice moved slowly with little erosive power. So there are few signs of the glaciation, other than a gentle rounding of the contours. The exception is the bowl below Cautley Crags. Just after the Devensian ice had melted, a short reversal of the climatic improvement caused a mini Ice Age, starting 11,000 years ago and only lasting 800 years. Lake District glaciers never reached the Howgills, and only a few snow fields built up on the higher Dales peaks. But the Cautley Crags valley faces north-east, where it could catch snow blown over the ridge on the west wind, to accumulate out of reach of the strongest of the sun's

A carpet of snow picks out the drystone walls of Wharfedale and also the stark overhanging cliff of Kilnsey Crag, where the edge of the limestone fells was cut off by an Ice Age glacier.

heat. So it is likely that a little corrie glacier grew and deepened the bowl beneath the Crags, though only flowing a few hundred yards down valley before it melted away.

So right up to 10,000 years ago, ice was fashioning the park's landscape. Not only did it scour the dales and trim the bedrock of the hills, but it also dumped a lot of debris in its melt zones. Boulder clay, an unsorted chaos of clay, sand and boulders of all sizes, is the characteristic glacial deposit, and it blankets huge areas of the Dales. Its rather variable thickness is mostly less than fifteen feet, but is greater in the protected lee of some of the hills, notably along the south flank of Ingleborough.

Though a lot of the boulder clay is just dropped as the ice melts away, some of it has been overridden by the glaciers and moulded into low, rounded and streamlined hills known as drumlins. Brough Hill, the site of the Roman fort at Bainbridge, is a single large drumlin, and there are many more down the length of Wensleydale. Drumlins tend to occur in clusters, known as drumlin fields, and perhaps the finest in Britain creates the distinctive hummocky terrain all around Ribblehead. This splendid drumlin field reaches across upper Ribblesdale and

A white streak marks Cantley Spout, where a small stream tumbles into a precipitous ravine from the crags on the eastern side of the Howgill Fells.

up on to the slopes of Cam Fell, Birkwith and Cosh.

On the southern edge of Ingleborough, the broad shoulder of Norber has a grass cover broken by outcrops of white limestone. But scattered across it are scores of dark, angular, gritstone boulders each up to ten feet across. These are the famous Norber erratics. They were dropped by a glacier at the end of the Ice Age, and their rock (the distinctive ancient

Just one of the Norber erratics on the southern flank of Ingleborough. The ten-foot long block of dark rock was dropped by an Ice Age glacier and now stands on a little plinth of protected limestone.

greywacke) matches the outcrop in the floor of Crummack Dale just to the north. This proves their glacial origin, for no river could carry them uphill, and also demonstrates the local pattern of ice flow. A lobe of the Ribblesdale glacier spread across the Sulber Scars, dropped into and enlarged Crummack Dale, and then partly overrode Norber on its way south.

Glacial deposition in a different style has modified Kingsdale – that lesser known of the dales, tucked away north of Ingleton, which ranks as a geological classic. Across the dale mouth the soft contours of the Raven Ray barrier rise 100 ft (30 m). A natural bank of boulder clay, this is a terminal moraine, left at the snout of the Kingsdale glacier during its final retreat at the end of the Ice Age. The debris buried the old valley – which can still be recognized to the left of Thornton Force when viewed from downstream – and it provided a temporary dam across the valley until the postglacial river cut a new route through it.

Glacial development of the national park area ceased at the end of the Ice Age, but the landforms did not then remain unscathed. As the climate warmed, the Dales entered a new fluvial regime, of

Stained brown from their passage through the peat bogs of the high fells, the waters of the River Clough cascade over clean ribs of limestone at the western end of Garsdale. This point is on the Sedgwick Geology Trail.

erosion and deposition by rainwater and rivers. But water erosion takes place rather slowly, and requires the span of geological time to carve entire landscapes. In their brief 10,000 years, the postglacial rivers and streams have generally only achieved small-scale modification of the Dales landscape, which is still dominated by the dramatic landforms left by the rivers' glacial ancestors. Because water is a more subtle erosive agent than ice, it has etched the landscape into a wealth of detail with a sensitive response to rock type.

Within the river channels themselves, the bedrock exercises a major influence. Nearly all the narrow rocky gorges and the entrenched sections of cascades are in limestones; thin bedded sequences of this rock create the lovely river-bed scenery of upper Dentdale, as well as the staircase of tumbling water through Gayle in Wensleydale. Between each little fall on both the River Dee and Gayle Beck, shale provides the contrasting weakness eaten out by the churning water, but, on its own, shale provides only valleys which are rather wide and featureless. The gritstone is another tough rock which survives as ledges and vertical walls even when undercut by a river; the rocky ravine of the Strid is the best known, where the Wharfe happens to have breached a strong grit bed, cutting its narrow channel up to thirty feet deep.

Outside the immediate river beds, limestone is still the most influential rock, and we shall return to its unique karst landscape. Water has also responded dramatically to the contrasting rocks of the Yoredale sequences. The broad outlines of the terraces which dominate Yoredale country were established beneath the glaciers: ice plucking levered out blocks of limestone or sandstone which was loosely founded on the shale, and then stripped down to the next strong bed. Postglacial water completed the process, washing away the weathered shale and undercutting the terrace edges. Now, the Yoredale terraces have made many Dales hillsides into veritable staircases, and their streams consequently drop over innumerable waterfalls.

Wensleydale is the heartland of waterfall country, and pride of place must go to Hardraw Force. It is a classic, overhanging Yoredale waterfall, 90 ft (27 m) high; it has a limestone lip, sandstone below, and its bottom forty feet into the softer shale, where the undercut shelters the dry footpath behind the

cascade. The force exists where the beck meets a
rock step as it tumbles into the Wensleydale glacial
trough; it is higher than it might have been because
the beck has been deflected a little east by a tail of
glacial boulder clay now forming Smithy Hill, and
this kept it out of an easier, lower line. Most
Wensleydale streams cascade over a Yoredale
limestone somewhere down their course, and
Whitfield Gill, just west of Askrigg, drops over two
spectacular waterfalls.

Though the cascades on the Yoredale rocks are
conspicuous in the Yorkshire Dales, there are many
others in different environments – the national park
is singularly well endowed with waterfalls. The
Aysgarth Falls are essentially due to retreat from
the step in the limestone valley floor where
Wensleydale hangs above the glacially
overdeepened Bishopdale. Even deeper glacial
excavation scoured the bowl into the east side of the
Howgill Fells, and let a north-flowing beck tumble
sideways down Cautley Spout. With a total, broken
drop of 600 ft (180 m), this is a rather spectacular
glacial stream diversion. Different again is Thornton
Force, that most beautiful of waterfalls at the mouth
of Kingsdale; it has formed where the beck dropped
back into its ancestral preglacial valley after being

Wain Wath Force is just
one of the low waterfalls
formed where the infant
River Swale cascades
over strong beds of
Yoredale rock near the
little village of Keld.

deflected round the Raven Ray terminal moraine, and the limestone lip creates the fine overhang above the weaker slates. Downstream, Pecca Falls, along with the rest of the waterfalls in both the Ingleton glens, are over resistant greywackes.

Add to these the falling streams below ground in the karst, and the Yorkshire Dales can present a splendid catalogue of contrasting waterfalls. Many of these owe part of their origin to their glacial heritage, but the keen observer can also recognize some other features. Hardraw Force has retreated over 250 yards up its ravine since glacial times; yet the present modest beck hardly seems capable of this much erosion. And, into the limestone, Gordale Scar is a massive gorge totally out of balance with a rather tiny beck. Both these owe their scale to a period of dramatic erosion by abrasive, sediment-laden meltwater.

For thousands of years Ice Age glaciers of the Yorkshire Dales were in an overall melting environment. Every summer, huge torrents of meltwater were produced from the glaciers and from more temporary snowfields. Meltwater rivers pouring from the glacier snouts are easily imagined. So are meltwater streams on the hills between the glaciers, perhaps kept at a high-level by deflecting barriers of ice; that conspicuous little channel at Capon Hall, crossing the Pennine watershed south of Fountains Fell, is a perfect example of high level meltwater erosion. But there was also subglacial water in torrents hidden away beneath slow moving ice, fed by crevasse water and scouring the bedrock beneath. Meltwater, both beneath and outside the glaciers, played a crucial role in the evolution of the Dales landscape.

Hardraw Force is completely postglacial, but for the first thousand years of its life the beck was augmented by massive meltwater flows, and a major part of the retreat back into the ravine dates from that short phase. In the case of Gordale Scar, there was probably more erosion by subglacial water. It can be difficult to distinguish the results of water erosion below or outside the glacier, but, either way, meltwater can quickly carve a deep gorge. Then when the climate warms, the gorge is left out of balance with its new environment, and in the case of limestone is preserved intact as the new erosive drainage goes underground. Meltwater carved nearly all the gorges in the Yorkshire Dales limestone. Gordale Scar, and Trow Gill on Ingleborough, are the best known. The Watlowes

Just north of Hawes, Hardraw Force is ninety feet high, with its waters dropping clear from an overhanging lip in the horizontal Yoredale rocks.

and Malham Cove are comparable, but they are features of the karst which we will return to later.

Lakes are not normal features of a fluvial regime; rivers tend to either fill them with deltas, or drain them by eroding their outlets. So there has to be a special story behind each lake. Malham Tarn exists partly because of the damming by the ice sediments, and partly because it sits in its own overdeepened basin. The park's only other sizeable lake, Semer Water, is also retained by a natural dam, this time a terminal moraine of boulder clay. But Semer Water is only a shadow of its former self; when the ice first retreated, the meltwater lake reached three miles up Raydale, but the upper end is now all filled with sediment. Other lakes have gone completely. There was one in front of Kilnsey Crag, dammed by the bedrock rise at Mill Scar Lash; now it is filled with sediment, leaving the very flat valley floor between Kilnsey and Conistone. Kingsdale had an even larger lake, and there was a tiny one in the bowl below Cautley Crags. Both were dammed by terminal moraines.

The end of the Ice Age was a turning point in the Dales' evolution. The glaciers melted, and so did the ground ice. Deep frozen during the Ice Age, the ground thawed from the surface downwards, and there was a critical phase when ground ice still survived below a wet, thawed surface layer. Saturated soil which could not drain was very unstable on the slopes. Soil creep, slumping and earth flows were common; either side of Cautley Crags debris flows mantle almost the entire hillsides. And there was even more severe movement – a huge landslide gouged the western face of Ingleborough, and another left Hooker Mill Scar on the western slope of Kisdon Hill. There are so many old flows and slides in the Dales; recognize them by the lumpy ground picked out by low light at a clear dawn or sunset. But they move no more; since the ground ice all melted, the soils have drained and the slopes are now stable.

The glaciers died, the lakes came and went, the hillsides moved and stopped; such was the demise of the Ice Age. But the changes also saw progress on two major fronts. New plants colonized, new soils developed and the landscapes began to resemble the green panoramas of the modern Dales. And as the limestone thawed, the streams sank into its open fissures, and the caves and karst added their unique characteristics to the national park.

Lying in the broad trough of Raydale, Semer Water is ponded behind a natural dam of glacial sediment across its northern end, on the right is this view from near Stalling Busk.

3 **Karst and caves of the limestone**

The Yorkshire Dales National Park was designated largely because of the limestone. A fundamental aim of the park was to include, and thereby protect, recognize and appreciate, the spectacular limestone scenery of the Dales. Malham and Gordale, Ingleborough and Gaping Gill, the caves and the karst – they are all features of the limestone. This rock provides the character of the park; but then limestone is a dominant influence almost wherever it occurs, because it forms the distinctive landscape of karst.

A karst landscape is one characterized by underground drainage, so it has sinkholes and caves while many of its valleys are dry or blind. The finest karst is formed on limestone, and Britain's finest is in the Yorkshire Dales.

Perhaps the most distinctive features of the Dales karst are the acres of bare white limestone pavement. The little strip of pavement at the top of Malham Cove fascinates countless visitors. Far more extensive, and as barren as a lunar landscape, are the huge pavements of Southerscales Scars and Scales Moor, which were scraped clean by the Chapel-le-Dale glacier; and therein lies their origin. Any strong rock can be scraped clean by a glacier; but in 10,000 years of postglacial history, most rocks weather to create a veneer of soil, and the glacial ancestry is lost. But the solutional removal of the limestone ensures that no mineral soil is formed, and the rock pavement survives. Glacial in origin and karstic in preservation, the pavements identify the Dales landscape as a glaciokarst.

Since the glaciers retreated, solution by water from both rainfall and impermanent organic soils has lowered the pavement surface. The erratic boulders of Norber now stand on plinths of limestone which they protect from rainfall and subsequent corrosion; each plinth stands about a foot higher than the exposed limestone and provides a very tangible demonstration of the rate of surface lowering. Rain and soil water has also etched into the pavements and widened the fractures into open fissures, locally known as

The superb limestone pavements of Souther-scales Scars on the northwest side of Ingleborough. Widely spaced joints in the bedrock have left large clints between the deep grike fissures.

grikes. Between the grikes stand the clints, unjointed blocks of limestone fretted by the deep solutional runnels often known as karren.

The stronger beds of limestone form the broadest pavements with the largest clints, and also provide the scars and low cliffs which rib many of the dale sides. Plucked clean by the passing glacier, White Scars and Twisleton Scars are among the finest, facing each other across Chapel-le-Dale.

One of nature's great disappearing tricks is performed by rainfall on the limestone pavements: it is swallowed into the open fissures. In some places it can be heard trickling away below ground, but then it is out of earshot and out of sight until it reappears in a valley-floor spring perhaps many miles away. Through the span of geological time, between the Ice Ages and since the last one, some fissures have been widened enough to swallow whole streams. Mossdale Beck disappears into a cliff high on Conistone Moor; the water from Malham Tarn sinks silently into its bed before reaching the Watlowes valley; there's a ring of over a hundred sinks around Ingleborough, including the great shaft of Gaping Gill which swallows Fell Beck; and tiny streams from a bog on Great Shunner Fell sink into the beautifully fluted shafts of the Buttertubs.

What goes in must come out, and all the sinking water returns to daylight at springs, which in some cases can also be open cave mouths. The Buttertubs water re-emerges from a little cave just 100 yards away and 100 feet lower down the fell; but the Mossdale water only emerges from the pool of Black Keld, in the floor of Wharfedale three miles away and 740 feet lower than the sink.

Most spectacular of the Dales sinkholes are the great potholes, and best known of all is Gaping Gill. Fell Beck drains eastern Ingleborough and then disappears into Gaping Gill, plunging 340 ft (103 m) down Britain's highest unbroken waterfall. The vertical shaft bells out in its lower part into a magnificent chamber over 500 ft (150 m) long and 100 ft (30 m) high and wide. Further north on Ingleborough, Alum Pot is only 200 ft (60 m) deep but is much more impressive from the surface viewpoint; its wider shaft offers awe-inspiring vertical panoramas of underground rock. Over on Pen-y-ghent, and very close to the Pennine Way, Hunt Pot is the textbook example of a Yorkshire pothole. A small stream drops over its wide lip and the curtain of spray dissolves into the blackness, heightening the mystery of what lies below.

In wet weather, a powerful stream cascades into the rocky chasm of Hull Pot, and then sinks into its floor of boulders and cobbles. Hull Pot lies close to Hunt Pot on the west side of Pen-y-ghent.

In reality, the potholes are just the most dramatic entrances to the caves. Hidden from view, but an integral component of the karst, cave passages lace the limestone throughout the national park. Every stream that sinks flows through a cave to its rising, and there are many more caves fed just by percolation water or left high and dry by ancient streams. A cave starts its life as a chance line of fractures. Water eats away the walls until it is an open fissure and then a cave passage of substantial size. A cave may be a narrow rift with a trickle of water; it may be a tunnel thirty feet across strewn with massive boulders; it may have an underground river swirling through lakes and crashing over waterfalls in the inky blackness. Water makes a passage larger, but it is a perversity of nature to also fill in cave passages. A stream may deposit banks of sand or mud, while dripping percolation water deposits calcite to form stalactites, stalagmites and flowstone. There is endless variety in the Dales caves.

At any time a cave stream may find a new route through the limestone, and abandon its earlier passage. Unlike a surface stream whose old profile is destroyed by subsequent erosion, an ancient cave is preserved underground and becomes a valuable record of past events. Within the national park there are innumerable fossil caves, mostly abandoned at high level when drainage adjusted to the lowering dale floors. The age of the caves can be determined from the traces of radioactive uranium in their stalagmites. A single stalagmite may form in 10,000 years, but some in the Dales caves are over a third of a million years old.

The show caves of Ingleborough Cave and Stump Cross Caverns are both segments of fossil passage

The warren of cave passages and the underground river of Gaping Gill beneath the southern slopes of Ingleborough.

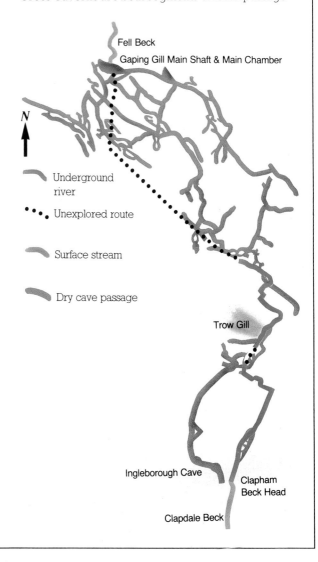

Fell Beck

Gaping Gill Main Shaft & Main Chamber

N

Underground river

Unexplored route

Surface stream

Dry cave passage

Trow Gill

Ingleborough Cave

Clapham Beck Head

Clapdale Beck

abandoned perhaps half a million years ago.
Ingleborough Cave once carried the main river
from Gaping Gill, and both caves were once full of
water, but now the main streams are at lower levels.

Each show cave is just a segment of an
underground network. A cave system may have
many streamways, perhaps converging at depth on
a major underground river, and interconnected by

The stalactite-draped roof
and the sloping floor of
broken rock are both
signs of the considerable
age of the Battlefield
Chamber inside White
Scar Cave, Ingleborough.

old passages remaining from bygone drainage
routes. Kingsdale is drained by a splendid cave
system, with dozens of streams feeding the
underground river which emerges from Keld Head.
There are seven miles of passages beneath the
eastern slopes of Gragareth, including long stream
routes, numerous waterfalls and the great shafts of
Rowten Pot. More passages carry streams from
Whernside right beneath the Kingsdale floor, but
these flooded tunnels are not yet fully explored and
mapped. Currently just outside the park boundary,
the Ease Gill Cave System is Britain's largest with
over thirty three miles of passages beneath the
western flanks of Gragareth.

With so much drainage underground, it is hardly
surprising that some valleys in the Yorkshire Dales
are dry. Conistone Dib, down into Wharfedale, and
the valley off southern Ingleborough below Gaping
Gill are typical karstic dry valleys. Both were
carved by meltwater when the ground was frozen
and the caves were still blocked by ice at the ends
of the Ice Ages. The gorge of Trow Gill was then cut
by waterfall retreat on the steeper slope down into
Clapdale. It is a popular misconception that
limestone gorges are collapsed caverns, a theory

The towering limestone cliffs of Gordale Scar were cut by torrents of meltwater at the end of the Ice Age. Now they hide just a little stream whose waterfalls are lost deep in the shadows.

based on their almost exclusive occurrence in cavernous rock. But they are just cut by surface rivers. The restriction of the finest gorges to limestone is a feature of their preservation since the Ice Age, because the modern erosive drainage has gone underground.

Gordale Scar is a most spectacular gorge nearly 500 ft (150 m) deep. It too was cut by meltwater cascading down the steep slope picked out along the Middle Craven Fault. In the depths of the Scar, the famous rock bridge is an underground short-cut, but there never has been a roof spanning the gorge to create a grand cave. A mere shadow of the erosive torrents of the past, Gordale's present stream is depositing great banks of banded calcite called tufa, both within the Scar and downstream at Janet's Foss.

The Malham Cove story is a little more complex. The tarn sits on a faulted block of impermeable slate beneath the limestone, and its outlet water is lost at the Water Sinks, just after crossing the North Craven Fault on to the limestone. The sinks are choked with stones, and the cave below is unexplored, but the water re-emerges largely at Aire Head, downstream of Malham village, and also

Malham Cove – cut by ice, trimmed by an ancient waterfall, and now just with a flooded cave at its foot.

partly at the foot of the cove. In the melt stages of the Ice Ages, the caves were still blocked by ice, and meltwater cut the Watlowes, a beautiful rocky valley which is now almost permanently dry. Its water cascaded 230 ft (70 m) over Malham Cove and must have made a splendid sight at the time. The vertical limestone wall of the cave is however much wider than its Watlowes feeder. It was largely cut by ice, was trimmed by waterfall retreat, was even undercut a little by the water resurging at its foot, and was then preserved by being left high and dry. It is a complicated history, but perhaps that is the main reason that Malham Cove is unique.

4 **Prehistory and the first impact of man**

With the slow warming of the climate, the Yorkshire Dales were probably clear of the main Ice Age glaciers before 13,000 years ago. Desolate wastes of rock and glacial debris were soon colonized by mosses and grasses, with new plant species spreading from the south with the migrating zones of warmer weather. A tundra landscape may have lasted a few thousand years, as the climatic improvement was at first hesitant, but then conditions improved to approach those of today around 10,000 years ago. Tundra matured into grassland and heath, and then trees transformed the scene..Birch came first, then pine, followed by hazel, each into the dales and then spreading up the hills until woodland covered almost the entire area of the national park. With the plants came the animals; first the reindeer over the snows, then wolves, bear, more deer and many smaller species.

These were not the first animals to colonize the Dales. Around 140,000 years ago, wolverine and reindeer had roved across an earlier tundra, and some had fallen down fissures in the limestone; sadly for them, but fortunately for us, their remains survived, sealed in the inner passages of Stump Cross Cave.

So the immigrants of 12,000 years ago were just reinvading the territory of their ancestors after the last Ice Age interruption. But there were changes: there was no mammoth, for this was extinct; there was no hippo, for it was too cold; and there was man.

Stone Age man was a bit late in coming to the Yorkshire Dales. He had been in southern Britain for a long time, but probably first settled the bleak Pennine hills on any significant scale at the very end of the Paleolithic period, around 9000 BC. The limestone country was the main attraction, where he lived in the caves, fished in the many small lakes and hunted and gathered in the forests. His carved antler tools have been found in Victoria Cave, and traces of his passing are in many other caves along the southern edge of the national park. After more than a thousand years of this primitive activity, the climate again improved, the forest thickened and

the animal life changed, and new migrants from the south heralded the Mesolithic period.

Evolution, of both natural vegetation and cultural aspects, proceeds very slowly, but 2,000 years of continually improving, warmer and drier climates followed those rather cold conditions of the Paleolithic. The forest cover spread with the warmth; hazel grew to dominate on the limestone plateaux, while oak and elm thickened in the dales.

The Mesolithic hunters roamed the rich woodlands and open ridges. Their flint tools, scrapers, blades and spear barbs have been found widely. Most lived in migratory groups and a few camp sites have been found, at Malham Tarn and on the high moors of Tan Hill, the latter perhaps an indication of the more amenable climate of the times. Their temporary shelters were of wood, hide and turf, so there is little to survive the passing of time. Though they left few tangible remains, the Mesolithic people may have left a more permanent impact with their early attempts at woodland clearance. Burning and cutting the forest back, they created open land for their animals. The loss of the trees' massive thirst left the ground wetter; and the exposed soil was leached to form hard pans in the

Victoria Cave, just east of Settle, was almost full of sediment before it was excavated in the last century. The dig revealed bones of mammoth, left from the colder climates of the Ice Ages, and also of rhino and hippo who lived in the area during warmer periods between the glaciations.

lower layers and so reduce the drainage. Both processes effectively created bog.

Later Mesolithic times were characterized by the great expansion of peat bog, though only a little of this was due to man. Between roughly 6000 and 4000 BC, the climate hit an optimum of warm and wet conditions. Alder and lime added to the deciduous woodland within the dales, but the high plateaux were too wet for forest, and the trees declined under the advance of the blanket bog. Only the well-drained limestone slopes evaded the bog and kept a woodland cover of hazel, birch and oak on their thinner soils.

The woodland dales and moorland bogs were inherited by the Neolithic people. They were the first real farmers, and also had permanent home sites and luxuries such as household pottery. For 2,000 years they thrived, until bronze eventually took them out of the Stone Age.

Most Neolithic people had houses of timber and turf, which have left little trace, but a few lived in some of the more comfortable caves, such as Foxholes, a fine rock shelter in Clapdale even adorned with a defensive outer wall. Some people temporarily occupied Victoria Cave and various others along the southern limestone margin. But the main use of the caves was for burial; above Wharfedale, Dowkerbottom Cave has a grave cut in stalagmite.

With so many ready-made graves available, burial mounds are rare in the Yorkshire Dales; but a few monuments were built. At the head of Pen-y-ghent Gill, Giant's Grave was an important burial site with chambers beneath an earth mound 50 ft (15 m) across. A rather flattened mound survives today with a few up-ended clints recognizable as the chamber walls. It was probably late in Neolithic times that the first henges were built. Castle Dykes is the prime example in the national park, standing high on the shoulder between Wensleydale and Bishopdale. It has a circular earthbank nearly 200 ft (60 m) in diameter, which was probably little more than a viewing platform. An inner ditch separates it from the central mound where the ceremonies were performed – though if standing stones were once part of the monument, no signs remain. Now just a grassy bank grazed by cattle, Castle Dykes recalls an early phase of settlement in the Yorkshire Dales well north of the favoured limestone belt. It is now one of the many ancient monuments given special protection status within the national park.

Organized enough to build a great henge, the Neolithic people were clearly more than nomadic hunters. Their later houseware was characterized by beautifully shaped clay beakers which have been found in many of the Dales caves, and they also had good flint knives. They truly farmed the land and kept domesticated animals in woodland clearings around permanent homesteads. The

Incomplete snow cover picks out the circular earth banks of the Castle Dykes henge, and also the much younger drystone walls crossing the fell between Wensleydale and Bishopdale.

record of pollen, preserved in the peats and bogs, shows increasing use of grain crops on land just cleared of forest. Some clearances were temporary, but others were permanent, and the continuing loss of trees set a trend which has been maintained in the Yorkshire Dales for the succeeding 5,000 years. The Neolithic farmers increased it, but there were not many of them and it is debatable how much they achieved, for nearly all their land has since been reworked. Perhaps the great tract of Romano-British fields north of Grassington hides a Neolithic ancestry; in which case this must be among the earliest of the limestone grasslands, which distinguish the southern part of the national park.

The Bronze Age did not start at a given date, but rather crept in. Though bronze probably first came to the area around 2500 BC, the pastoral farmers of the Pennine hills must have continued for generations without knowledge of the new metal. Bronze Age settlement was more extensive in the Craven area than in the northern dales, because the people still preferred the dry limestone country. This choice may have become a curse in the middle Bronze Age when a spell of warmer drier climate may have left the ground too dry. Combined with a steady population increase this prompted a spread on to the grit moors. The treeline was high on the warmer fells, and the spread of the farming promoted a massive attack on the natural forest. Large patches of clearance emerged, and then, around 1000 BC, the climate deteriorated and the blanket bog expanded again in a cool, wet spell. The decline of the forests took yet another irretrievable step.

Not all the cleared land was for open grazing. Cereal and flax were rotated with pasture in small fields within the shelter of the dales. Remains of the field systems have been recognized in Swaledale where they were overlain by the Iron Age earthworks near Reeth, and surely there were more whose traces were destroyed by later ploughing.

Ceremonial and burial sites provide the best evidence of Bronze Age activity. The henge at Castle Dykes was probably still in use; a smaller, similar, earthbank henge at Yarnbury, above Grassington, may be of Bronze Age origin, but could have Neolithic ancestry. Down the valley at Rylstone, a round barrow has yielded a wooden coffin, and there seems to have been a trend away from caves as simple burial sites. A number of stone

The ring of broken wall-stone on the floor of Langstrothdale close to Yockenthwaite may have been an ancient religious site, but was probably just a tomb enclosure.

circles may be of similar age, though their religious significance may be questioned.

Man's ability to modify his environment took a leap forward when much more efficient axes and ploughs could be made from iron. The spread of the new metal was again slow, and the remote upland groups were the last to benefit, but the Iron Age really opened in the Yorkshire Dales around 600 BC. The climate improved from its cold wet phase at the end of the Bronze Age, but already the bog and heath was firmly established on the higher fells, and the summit landscapes were much as they are today. There was still plenty of woodland within the dales and on the steeper slopes, but patchy clearance was relentlessly continued.

The Iron Age population is often considered to have been a mixture of the tribal groups known as Brigantes, who were local in origin, and immigrant people who came in increasing numbers from the first century BC onwards. Though the limestone of the southern dales was still the popular settlement area, there was much more activity now in the northern dales. Above Wensleydale there were communities high on Addlebrough and Pen Hill, where traces of their huts and fields can still be seen. There were stilt houses in the shallows of Semer Water; flint arrowheads suggest a Neolithic ancestry, but the houses appear to be Iron Age.

Swaledale also had its Iron Age settlements with well-ordered fields still leaving their traces on the side of Calver Hill, west of Reeth, but the valley was also of more importance. Maiden Castle, set on a commanding shoulder south-west of Reeth was a seat of power and influence. Cut into the hillside, its levelled circle over 200 ft (60 m) across is protected by a rampart which even today stands 15 ft (5 m) above its outer ditch. Just a mile to the east, the dykes between Grinton and Fremington are a pair of rampart and ditch structures right across the valley floor and lower slopes of Swaledale, and most of their lengths are still clearly visible. These massive features were not hastily built defences, but were prestige developments which suggest a well-organized community. Though they appear to pre-date the Roman threat, their exact age and purpose remains a mystery. There is similar doubt over the origins of Tor Dyke above Wharfedale. Its mile of ramparts, cleverly incorporating a natural limestone scar, appears to defend Coverdale.

The limestone region of the southern dales had numerous Iron Age settlements. With some large

Aerial view of the summit plateau of Ingleborough. The boundary ramparts of the Iron Age fort are clearly visible, and a few hut circles can be seen towards the near right.

areas cleared of woodland, the pastoral communities enclosed more and more fields around their huts, and these steadily grew into the vast tracts of Celtic fields which largely post-date the Roman interlude. The Brigantes tribes did not take kindly to the prospect of Roman domination and they took solace from their proximity to Ingleborough. The splendid flat cap of this imposing hill holds an Iron Age fort. Today's passing visitor hardly recognizes the ramparts which trace its rim, for these are now much degraded, and only from the air are the nineteen hut circles easily seen inside the ramparts. This was purely a defensive site, with no farming at such a high level, and its lofty isolation makes it Britain's highest Iron Age fort. It originates from early in the Iron Age, but was probably reoccupied by the Brigantes when Venutius led them in a last stand against the Roman invaders.

The Romans came to Britain in AD 43; they conquered the Vale of York in AD 71; and they subdued the Brigantes of the Yorkshire Dales in AD 74. The Roman fort of Virosidum, on the drumlin hill at Bainbridge, was the largest in the national park area, and was occupied for most of the period from AD 80 until the main withdrawal of 395. It may have garrisoned up to 500 soldiers in wood and stone buildings, but the site now only reveals grassed-over mounds and ramparts.

The Romans never colonized the Yorkshire Dales, but only controlled them by holding key points and routes. The Brigantes stayed in the high country, mainly on their small farms, but with some still living in the caves. Victoria Cave may have been occupied temporarily by metal-workers, but both it and nearby Attermire Cave were sacred sites which collected offerings of gold, silver, coins, pottery and even Roman material taken as battle trophy. The struggle against the Romans was valid, as captured Brigantes were probably taken as slaves to work the lead mines of Greenhow and Arkengarthdale.

While the hill tribes remained apart, the native farmers took to a peaceful co-existence with the Roman occupiers. Rural activity reached a zenith when there was no limit to the amounts of grain, meat and wool which could be supplied to the Romans, and which were probably partly exported along with the lead. The climate was generally as good as it is today, and the fields were carefully ordered, some being terraced with the first small lynchets for better arable management. The extent of the fields around Malham, still recognizable by their degraded wall lines, could support around 320 people, and that is about double today's population. Fields were rotated between cereal, vegetables and pasture, while cows and pigs grazed the uncleared woodland, though the destructive pigs were being steadily replaced by sheep.

After 300 years the Romans left, the hill tribes rejoined the lowland farmers, and the British people went into another two centuries of peaceful life in the Yorkshire Dales. It is even possible that they formed their own kingdom of Craven, tucked in between Northumbria, Elmet to the south-east, and Strathclyde to the west. Still the limestone country supported the densest settlement. Woodland covered the higher benches, the upper ends of the dales, and the narrower valley floors, but large areas were open fields, creating a ground texture some of which has survived today. The low grass-covered ridges which break so much of the modern pasture are the degraded remnants of ancient walls, of both fields and farms. They have survived well in the sheep-grazed grassland, though some are a little difficult to recognize, except from just the right angle, or when picked out by blown snow or the shadow of a low sun.

North of Grassington, perhaps Britain's finest stretch of 'Celtic' fields extends up the side of Wharfedale to beyond Kettlewell. The grassed banks trace many old fields, some with short lynchets, and in places closer patterns trace the old settlements.

Further north there is less known of British activity. Perhaps this is largely because the better sites on the dale floors have seen subsequent arable

Low evening sun picks out the grassy banks which are the remains of field walls and buildings from an ancient 'Celtic' settlement. These are at Hill Castles Scar, above Conistone, in Wharfedale.

ploughing, which would have destroyed the earlier features. Farmsteads on Addlebrough and Pen Hill were still occupied, and it is notable that settlements ranged up to 1,700 ft (500 m) in altitude. One on the north slope of Langstrothdale has an aspect so bleak and inhospitable at present that one is tempted to think the climate must have been better then than now

The basic style of British farming continued in the Yorkshire Dales with little change, until the arrival of the Angles, who infiltrated the park area around the year 620. By then much of the lower dale floors were arable land, while the limestone hills were good pasture or thin scrub; the extent of prehistoric farming was such that most of the limestone woodland was just secondary ash. The Angles continued the arable farming, grazed their animals through the upper woods, and cleared yet more of the riverside woodland; their descendants probably established the first of the nucleated villages which were the beginnings of the settlement pattern of today. More changes took place as the Pennines were settled by successive waves of Danes, Norse and ultimately the Normans. The Yorkshire Dales were carried into the medieval period of village growth, trade expansion and the steady transformation into the modern landscape.

After 10,000 years of man's occupation, the Dales finally lost the prehistoric traditions of life. Migrating hunting groups, cave dwellers and isolated hill tribes became memories of the past. Perhaps a single settlement at Ribblehead epitomizes the style this way of life had reached. Still clearly recognizable on the northern tip of the Ingleborough limestone are the lower stone walls of

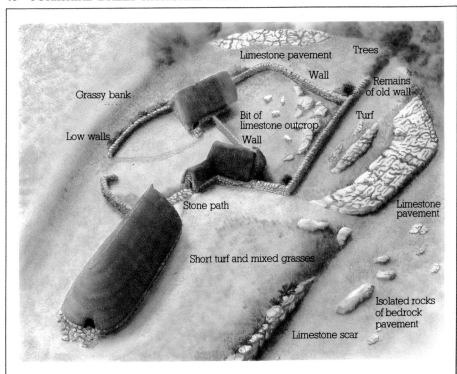

Grassy bank

Low walls

Limestone pavement

Trees

Wall

Remains of old wall

Bit of limestone outcrop

Turf

Wall

Stone path

Limestone pavement

Short turf and mixed grasses

Isolated rocks of bedrock pavement

Limestone scar

a house sixty feet long. It appears to have been in the Viking style, and coins date it to around 870. Excavation revealed bits of run lead and zinc, traces of iron, clay moulds and bits of enamel; it may have been a significant industrial site for its time, even though there are no mineral ores nearby. Outside, upended limestone slabs trace enclosure walls where stock was handled. Some of the stock pens surround bare limestone clints; the grass cover which they must have had at the time has been lost due to overgrazing and subsequent soil erosion.

So the people of Ribblehead were industrialists and traders who must have opened up lines of communication. Yet they were also farmers who were still unknowingly modifying the landscape through their simple methods.

A reconstruction of the settlement at Ribblehead, on the northern tip of Ingleborough, more than 1100 years ago.

5 The villages and the buildings

Where the Yorkshire Dales were once just wild upland, much of it is now a rural landscape integrated with a built environment of farms and villages. The transformation took hundreds of years, but an early landmark was the famous date of 1066 when English society was given a new order and purpose by the incoming Normans.

Through the Dark Ages up until 1066, the Yorkshire Dales was occupied by a polyglot mixture of different ethnic groups who had successively arrived in the area, not as invaders, but as immigrants. The Danes had come in 878, and the Norse had drifted in around 940. All these groups created clearings and farms on sites which often grew, much later, into villages. In some cases the names give a key to their history; the Norse had summer farms known as seters, and Appersett is one of four villages recalling the term in upper

Near the upper end of Swaledale, the little village of Thwaite has the walls and roofs of its houses, and its bridge, all built of local stone.

Wensleydale. There were few nucleated villages at this time, and most of the sites recorded in the famous Domesday Book of 1086 were no more than townships. These were just recognizable areas, subdivisions of parishes containing a scatter of farms, but their names have often survived to appear as the villages of today.

Domesday Book was the Norman survey of England, but its compilation followed a violent period in the north of the country. Notably in the Vale of York, but also in the adjacent uplands, including the Dales area, peasant revolts and local rebellions caused the Normans increasing trouble, and their response was the 'harrying of the North', from 1069 to 1071. This was little less than genocide, with wholesale killing of the local peasants, and a massive takeover by new Norman landlords. Total systematic slaughter was not easily achieved in the Pennine uplands, and many peasants did survive, though some areas were laid waste and totally depopulated.

Finally the Normans gained control, and held it with their strongholds, which became the centres of new settlement. Richmond was the prime example, and its castle, with parts dating to 1071 though largely rebuilt in 1160, is one of Britain's finest. Middleham was another on a smaller scale, but both these are now outside the national park.

Village growth was encouraged within the structure of Norman society, though it was a slow process in the thinly populated Dales. Some sites did grow in importance, and have thrived until today. Hunting forests were established in the upper parts of many of the dales. Buckden, Healaugh and Bainbridge evolved as forest villages, the latter beside the remains of the Roman fort, while Kettlewell, Askrigg and Reeth grew even faster as trading villages on the edge of the forests. The Norman churches were thinly spread, with huge parishes, and Grinton grew in stature with its church serving the whole of Swaledale. Other villages developed purely because of the natural advantages of their sites, and Arncliffe is the perfect example, occupying a drained gravel fan rising clear of the wet floor of Littondale.

A splendid feature of many villages is the green. Some may be inherited from the very first patterns of growth, and have been preserved through subsequent rebuilding of all the houses. Among the finest in the national park are Arncliffe and Linton in the south, and Bainbridge, West Burton and East

The remains of Bolton Priory have the stark skeleton of the unroofed chancel overlooking a lovely stretch of the River Wharfe.

Witton in the north. West Burton is a lovely village; it has never had a market or a church, though a township of the name featured in Domesday Book, and it still has fine old houses wrapped around its swathe of grass.

A driving force in the early development of the Yorkshire Dales was the power of the monasteries and the management of their huge estates. During times of religious popularity and support, the monasteries accrued their land by piecemeal donations from the Norman landlords; eventually most of the park area was in the hands of ten monasteries, though all but two of these lay outside the boundary. Bolton Priory is the notable exception, with its beautiful site on the banks of the Wharfe. Established by the Augustinians in 1155, it had estates reaching across into Airedale, and its twenty canons worked with over two hundred lay brethren, well integrated with the community. The core of the priory was built before 1300, and there were additions over the next 200 years. In 1539 its partial destruction, during the Dissolution, was ensured by the usual practice of deroofing, but the nave was preserved to remain as the village church.

Fountains Abbey was a major influence in the southern dales, owning most of the land between Fountains Fell and Langstrothdale. It had moorland sheep farms or granges such as Green Field, which is still only an isolated farm in upper Langstrothdale, but it also put Kilnsey on the map. This was the

Abbey's key grange, linked to the upland farms by
Mastiles Lane, and used for sheep shearing and
trading, with a handy sideline in thatching reeds
from the adjacent marsh.

In the north, Jervaulx Abbey owned much of
Wensleydale and also reached down to its horse
farm at Horton in Ribblesdale. Much of Swaledale
was owned by distant Bridlington Priory, and
elsewhere in the national park, large estates were
owned by the monasteries of Coverham, Furness,
Byland, Rievaulx, Sawley and Easby.

A market charter was a key stepping stone in the
growth of any village, and could have long lasting
effects. Richmond and Skipton won theirs around
1150, and both were based on Norman strongholds;
trade, wealth and power naturally accrued, and
they are still the leading service centres for most of
the national park. After 1200, there was a rash of
new market charters in the Dales; villages grew but
not all matured into the towns of today. Wensley
gained its charter in 1202, but it was only one of
many in competition, and its market declined in
1563 after it had been hard hit by the plague. Today
it lies in the shadow of Leyburn, which was a
latecomer with its market charter granted in 1684.
Kettlewell was another early market, well sited on
the edge of the Coverham, Fountains and Bolton
monastic estates; after a late boost through its local
mining, it too declined, in deference to Grassington.

Early markets at Settle, Sedbergh and
Grassington each thrived and continued to grow
through the next 700 years. But the tiny villages of
Clapham and Grinton lost the memories of their
market heydays into the sands of time. Even greater
contrast was provided by some sites which never
grew. Malham had a fine location, was surrounded
by monastic granges, had a huge annual drovers'
fair on Great Close, and later had its mining
interlude. But it remained small, almost waiting for
its tourist boom of today.

In those far-off days, few buildings had any real
permanence. Survival was only ensured with stone,
and this was restricted to castles, churches, the
monasteries, and the rare mansion. Most of the
Dales churches have seen subsequent rebuilding
with only small parts, and perhaps interior
stonework, surviving from the original. Wensley
church dates from around 1240, with a rebuild only
ninety years later, though its tower is of 1719; it has
splendid choir stalls dating from 1527, and a
beautifully carved wooden screen of similar age

Barden Tower was built as a forest hunting lodge just north of Bolton Priory in lower Wharfedale; though restored in 1638 it is now partly in ruins.

which was originally made for Easby Abbey but was rescued on the Dissolution.

The few large houses of this age were built with an eye to the defensive, and the prime example is Bolton Castle in Wensleydale. This was built as a home for the Scrope family in 1378, but with corner towers and curtain walls; sadly the north-east tower fell in 1761, prey to siege damage and a subsequent violent storm. Adjacent to the castle is the village of Castle Bolton, created at the same time. The church is the original, but the houses have all been rebuilt in the two rows fringing the elongate green.

The Dissolution of the monasteries around 1538 was a turning point in the history of the Yorkshire Dales, making a visual impact still conspicuous in the national park today. The monasteries themselves were closed and rendered useless by removing their roofs, and the shells were subsequently raided as a convenient source of building stone. Coverham Abbey, at the foot of Coverdale, was soon in ruins, and only a few arches stand today. Bolton Priory was the partly preserved exception, but there are scant remains of the two small Swaledale nunneries of Marrick and Ellerton.

The huge monastic estates were then sold off, in the first instance to the landed gentry and wealthy London merchants. Quickly the farms were resold to the sitting tenants – thereby creating a new population of freeholders. There was now the incentive to improve and refurbish the houses and

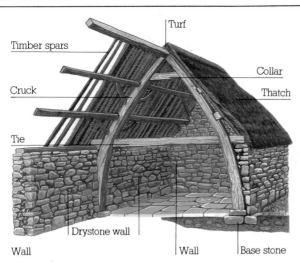

Timber spars

Turf

Collar

Cruck

Thatch

Tie

Drystone wall

Wall

Wall

Base stone

The distinctive structure of a Dales cruck barn has the pair of massive curved crucks, the steeply-pitched roof and only a narrow loft space.

farms, and, after a few generations in the Elizabethan climate of prosperity, it was possible to rebuild with stone. So the seventeenth century saw in the Yorkshire Dales a huge expansion of new stone buildings, many of which survive to form the farms and village cores of today and provide such distinctive features in the landscape of the Dales.

Until this time the typical farmhouse was of wood, probably without even stone foundations, and therefore having little of permanence. Some roofs were clay over branches, but most were thatched, and ling heather was much more common than reed; the crest line was often flaughts of turf sod. A distinctive structural style was in the use of crucks; these matching, or halved, curved tree limbs supported a steeply pitched roof. Size was limited by the available timber, and a normal span was about sixteen feet. A length of about twelve feet between crucks created a bay, which enclosed an area large enough for a family dwelling or to house two pairs of oxen. Adding a pair of crucks created another bay on a longer building, and the bay-size unit and the design of the longhouse were carried through into stone buildings no longer dependent on crucks.

In the seventeenth century the new freeholders' enthusiasm for better, more permanent houses of stone led to a whole new style of architecture. It was domestic-orientated, purposeful rather than ornamental, and dependent on locally available stone. This vernacular style, expressed in the ordinary cottages and farm buildings, still

Throughout the Dales, a flagstone roof is a common feature on the older buildings, here a farm near Muker, in Swaledale.

characterizes the Yorkshire Dales, and is a local feature as distinctive as any in Britain.

The traditional Dales farmhouse has limestone walls, with cornerstones and lintels of gritstone, and a flagstone roof. This very attractive combination of stones was imposed by the local geology, and has created a hallmark to the buildings almost throughout the national park. In most areas limestone is the ubiquitous strong rock, but it is not easily worked. Consequently, rough uneven blocks are used for the main walls, always as two mortared skins, with a rubble or chip infill, and held together by occasional larger stones placed as 'throughs'.

Gritstone was needed for the finishings as it was more easily worked into squared blocks or beams. It normally had to be carried further, often from small hilltop quarries; only in lower Wharfedale, around Burnsall, was there local grit to use for the entire walls. The grit was excellent for the cornerstones or 'quoins', rectangular blocks carefully set and meshed with the limestone wallwork by being laid in alternate orientations. Stone framing for the recessed windows incorporated more delicate masonry. Sills and lintels were of grit, except where budget imposed cheaper local limestone. Side supports may be stacked quoins, but more desirable were grit mullions, often carved into a splayed column, though the later trend was for flat faces.

Doorways are highlights of the Dales architecture. Supported on either stacked quoins or large jambs where available, the doorheads were mostly carved gritstone; ornamentation often included two or three initials – the Christian names and perhaps the surname of the new occupiers – and also a date. Though the dates can refer to a marriage, or may come from an older house, interpretation can yield a fair timetable of this phase of stone building. In the town of Settle, the surviving doorhead dates range from 1602 to 1840, with a peak around 1660. Further up the Dales, the overall range is comparable but the peak is around 1700. The picture is one of a wave of building activity sweeping up the Dales, as techniques, traditions and even wealth slowly migrated from town to country.

The new roofing material was flagstone. Earlier roofs needed a steep pitch to be weatherproof with the heather thatch, and also to fit the cruck profile. Then load-bearing walls of stone permitted use of the modern tie-beam truss roof with a lower pitch rendered good by the heavy flags.

Even with the new techniques in stone, house dimensions followed the old cruck-bay unit of sixteen feet by twelve feet, and most houses were two-bay. A single downstairs living room was normal, maybe with another parlour/bedroom, and there were bed chambers upstairs. There was usually no separate kitchen, and cooking was on the main fireplace in a gable end. Porches were rare, and there was no space for them in crowded

West New House, at the head of Bishopdale, is a splendid laithe house dating from 1635, with barns tagged on the end of a three-bay family unit, it is now a listed building, protected for the future.

villages, so the front door opened directly into the living room. Cruck designs had gone out of fashion before 1700 and survived only in barns, some of which had stone gable ends and still show the old profile through the subsequent conversion to a truss roof. Extra bays or attached barns added length. Originally this formed the longhouse, with animals and people in sections of the same building; but this evolved into the laithe house, with stone walls between the animal byre and the two-storey family quarters.

Many farm and village houses have survived,

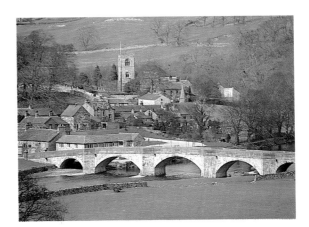

The gritstone village of Burnsall with its splendid bridge across the River Wharfe.

through modifications and additions, from the great building phase of 1630 to 1730. The blend of limestone, grit and flag is now a feature of the national park, but there are variations on the theme. Perhaps Burnsall was the most fortunate of villages, surrounded by the best of the gritstone which was easily worked and mellow in appearance. Soon after 1600 the church was rebuilt, the bridge was renewed, and the school was opened; they all survive. Exploiting the grit was a forerunner of new techniques which brought in further changes in style and really saw the end of the Yorkshire Dales vernacular.

The Fountaine Hospital in Linton – not a medical centre, but six almshouses – was a leader of the new wave in 1721. It relied on sawn gritstone, ashlar, enlivened by projecting quoins in the Palladian style derived from distant Italy. Prestige building followed the trend and evolved into the Georgian style. Sawn stone permitted monolithic door jambs and taller windows with longer mullions, and the

inherited dimensions of the cruck bay were at last forgotten in a rash of large country houses. Marske Hall in Swaledale dates from 1750, with Swinninthwaite Hall near Wensley from 1792, and Oughtershaw Hall followed a little later in the wilds of Langstrothdale.

Contemporary with the bold new houses were some sensitive restorations of old churches. Arncliffe had a timber church in Saxon times, with the first stone version before 1100; rebuilt in both the sixteenth and eighteenth centuries it is still a lovely building on a splendid site beside the Skirfare. A classic of the distinctive Pennine Perpendicular style is Hubberholme church in Wharfedale, with its long low nave and narrow square tower. Restored in 1863 it retains some of its original stonework and also has intact its magnificent oak rood loft dating from 1558. The old vicarage did however change, and is now the George Inn.

The eighteenth century in the Yorkshire Dales saw major changes through the Enclosures and the Industrial Revolution, both coming towards its end. The Enclosures started around 1770 and led to the major share of the drystone walls which are still so

Almost in the middle of the green at Linton, the old stone bridge has a lovely low arch across the beck.

conspicuous; many of the field barns date from the same time, but we shall return later to the evolution of the farming in the park.

Heavy industry never came to the Yorkshire Dales, but textile mechanization was a major influence. Wool was a local resource, but then the cotton industry spread to the Dales when the Leeds and Liverpool Canal reached Gargrave and Skipton in the 1780s. Water-powered mills had long been a feature of many villages, and through the nineteenth-century textile era they had a heyday within a series of changes of use. Most villages started with corn mills; Linton, in Wharfedale, was no exception, and then in 1780 it had a new mill for worsted; in 1840 this changed to cotton spinning, and then after a rebuild in 1901 reverted to worsted until its closure in 1959. Across the river, Grassington's Low Mill successively handled corn, cotton, silk, flax, soap and timber, before being turned into housing. These two perhaps typified the dozens of mills in the Dales, with almost every village having its own and thus being drawn through a period of prosperous expansion.

In the heart of Arkengarthdale, the knot of houses forms the village of Langthwaite, while the few houses of High Green stand across the valley.

Through the nineteenth century, the village of Dent was an important centre, twice the size of Sedbergh, though still dependent on the market at Kendal. It was renowned for its knitting products, notably the worsted stockings made from locally carded wool. Arten Gill was the site of a wool mill built in 1780, but in 1810 this took an unusual change to cutting and polishing a rather good local marble, though it was closed by 1900. Knitting was a major cottage industry in a belt spreading east from Dentdale, with other centres at Gayle and Reeth.

From villages come towns, and Skipton and Hawes grew to have major roles. For Skipton this was not new; it had long been a key centre. Between 1650 and 1700 its High Street was rebuilt, and the canal and the turnpikes came in the next century. Wool and cotton mills followed, and the town expanded with terraces of gritstone houses. Hawes was a relative latecomer, only gaining its market charter in 1700.

Other villages remained small, and Castle Bolton can claim to be the first estate village in the park area. Around 1800, East Witton was rebuilt by the Earl of Aylesbury with stone houses and the gardens faithfully matching an estate map of 1627; but five houses were originally sited on the green, and these were omitted, to the eternal benefit of the lovely village. At the same time, the Farrer family remodelled most of Clapham village, rebuilding houses, creating the lake and planting the magnificent woods.

Reaching across a substantial part of the national park, the mining industry was a great influence, largely between about 1720 and 1840. We will return to the mines, minerals and quarries later, but we must not forget those villages which grew, and declined, with the fortunes beneath the ground. Swaledale has the richest history from when its lead mines fed a total of twenty smelt mills in the boom years up to 1800. The tributary Arkengarthdale was a centre of activity, and Langthwaite grew in importance, while hamlets like Whaw and Eskleth developed from miners' homesteads.

Second only to Swaledale, Grassington was a centre of lead mining through the same period, when Wharfedale supported thirteen smelt mills. Kettlewell and Starbotton both grew with their mines and mills, and Grassington expanded as the main town in Wharfedale.

Population drifts are a feature of the mining industry, due to its rapid booms and declines. In the heady days up to 1800, Swaledale had 8,000 people, and now has only a fifth of that number. Coal mining was never on a scale to be a major influence, though the hamlet of Cotterdale may claim coal as its early motivation. Recently the shift has been to stone quarrying along the southern edge of the park, with growth at Ingleton, Horton and Grassington.

The greatest recent changes in the Dales have been related to modern transport. In 1901 the railway came to Grassington and put it within commuting distance from Bradford for the first time. Mobility eliminated the need for close-spaced market towns, and the main trade now is through Skipton, Richmond and Settle, all just outside the park. Sedbergh remains in the shadow of Kendal, and only Hawes has retained its importance.

Tourism leapt into significance with the coming of the railways, and Ingleton and Hardraw were two sites which felt the benefit of trainloads of visitors. Even with the Settle to Carlisle line, most of the park is an upland area, remote from rail access, and development had to wait for widespread car ownership. Today, the tourist industry is the one growth area within the national park. Visitor trade and associated craft industries are a significant aid to keeping some of the small villages alive. In the short summer season, tourism is a dominant theme, and perhaps Malham has taken the greatest impact.

Kettlewell is a lovely village almost free of modern development; its houses, inns and church stand either side of a beck tumbling down towards the River Wharfe.

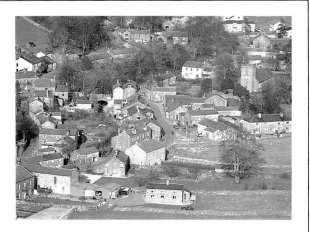

A sideline of the tourist industry has been the major recent growth of holiday homes. This is the one increasing house demand taking over from so many aspects in decline. Miners' cottages the length of Swaledale have become second homes or holiday lets for distant city dwellers. Farm mechanization and the associated migration of rural labour has released cottages throughout the park, but the holiday pressure is still not satisfied. The old mill at Airton is one of a number now developed into flats, and barn conversions are common in every dale. In the village of Kettlewell, half the houses are now just holiday occupancies. Change is rarely welcomed, but if the visitor industry keeps some of the lovely Dales houses occupied and free from ruin, then it cannot be all bad.

The houses, farms, mills and inns of the Yorkshire Dales have been over 300 years in their building. Another 700 years went into the siting of the villages, the wealth of fine old churches and a scatter of castles and monasteries. The result is a man-made environment largely in harmony with the natural splendours of the national park. Without it the Dales would be rather bleak. Its presence gives heart and soul to a lovely area of English highland, and there is no finer contrast than between a hamlet of beautiful stone houses and the wild open fells above.

6 **Road and rail**

The roads of the national park are much more than just the view from the car window, for they carry a long history which reflects the whole evolution of the Yorkshire Dales. A thousand years ago there were almost only footpaths; tracks, trails and rough roads grew from small beginnings; some of them evolved into the modern roads, while others stayed with a quieter role; and the modern enthusiasm for leisure footpaths brings the story full circle.

Superimposed on the erratic lines of prehistoric footpaths, the first proper roads, built to last, were made by the Romans. Within the park, the major Roman road is from Bainbridge to Ingleton; it is still recognizable, on the ground or on the map, by its bold straight lines, though today it poses in many forms. Labelled the Cam High Road, it rises from Bainbridge to Dodd Fell as a green track. With walls

Ruler-straight, the Roman road south from Bainbridge leaves Semer Water below, and climbs past Stalling Busk on its way over the high fells to Wharfedale.

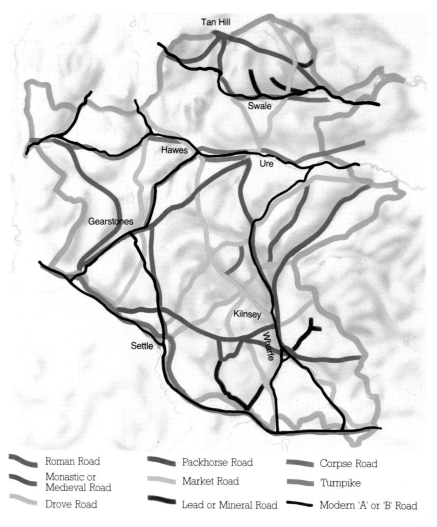

Roman Road	Packhorse Road	Corpse Road
Monastic or Medieval Road	Market Road	Turnpike
Drove Road	Lead or Mineral Road	Modern 'A' or 'B' Road

Roads of the Yorkshire Dales, ancient and modern. (Only the first or major use of the road is shown by colour.)

from a later era, and a surface largely grass, partly mud and with traces of stone foundations, this is typical of an ancient Dales routeway now retired and a pleasant walkers' trail. From Sleddale Head it has a strip of tar giving access to Cam Houses. Then west of the lonely farm, the Roman road is only a footpath, but with a new generation of traffic, as it is part of the Pennine Way except for its descent into Gearstones. From there to Ingleton it is a modern road, though just a quiet lane beneath Twisleton Scars where it is bypassed by the new road across the dale. West of Ingleton, and east of Bainbridge,

Boldly sweeping across Kilnsey Moor, the green track of Mastiles Lane was an important monastic route 700 years ago, but today is more used by walkers in search of peace and quiet.

the Roman road is lost. What was an ancient highway is today a road, a green track, a footpath and nothing. Time has wrought the changes.

The Roman roads, and the earlier field paths, probably changed little in a thousand years, but evolved in medieval times as new village growth demanded new routes. Among the longer routes of this new wave were the monastic tracks linking distant estates. Fountains Abbey, lying just east of the national park, had lands across the southern dales and into the Lake District. Its linking artery is best known as Mastiles Lane, that most splendid of green tracks across Malham Moor. Its line continues west to Thwaite Lane down into Clapham, and east of Kilnsey there was a wooden bridge over the Wharfe before it followed the line of the present motor road to Pateley Bridge.

These ancient tracks were narrow, rough, steep and hard. Their traffic was people carrying loads to market, packhorses, and droves of cows, sheep and geese; there was no leisure in walking in those days. Their sense of purpose kept them to direct lines, making them easy to recognize on modern maps where they contrast with the longer and easier lines of the modern roads. A market town as important as Settle had tracks radiating from it. One went to Malham, and stretches of its stone surface can still be seen in the Stockdale valley. A second went north-east to Arncliffe, largely on the course of the modern road, but with shorter higher lines above Langcliffe and over Knowe Fell. And a third went up Ribblesdale and over Ling Gill to join the Roman road.

The Arncliffe track continued to Starbotton and then almost over the top of Great Whernside to reach Nidderdale. This bold route is perhaps matched in splendour by the Bycliffe Road just to the south, which still offers a striking way across Conistone Moor. The section from Arncliffe to Starbotton was one of five tracks crossing the high ridge between Littondale and Wharfedale. They took the short routes, even though they climbed 1,000 feet or more, in marked contrast to the modern roads which stick to the dales floor. But all five routes survive today as footpaths which are still rights of way.

Some tracks had a more specific purpose. Swaledale had a Corpse Way, the last journey for those on their way to the mother church of Grinton with the dale's only burial ground. The Way looped high over the fells, and it survives as paths over Kisdon, above Ivelet, and across Low Row Pasture before descending to Feetham where the inn was a welcome halt for pall-bearers. Churches tended to be a focus for paths, and Gayle is linked direct to Hawes church by Bealer Bank. This is a flagged causeway across the meadows, mellowed into the landscape and providing a lovely walk; its careful construction may be a pointer for the national park footpaths of the future where unmade tracks suffer so much pedestrian erosion.

Building these early tracks was normally a piecemeal affair. Flagging was rare, but stone and gravel improved the softer ground, nicks were hammered through limestone scars and stone ports marked the way. These were the features that survived and can still be recognized on high and lonely fells. The costs of repairs were always a problem until an Act of Parliament in 1555 decreed that routeways were a parish responsibility, and, once defined, standards could improve.

Bridges were expensive items, and on major routes the costs were borne by the county. It is difficult to conceive that the main coaching route from London to Richmond came via Skipton, up Wharfedale and over into Coverdale, bringing

trade and support to what is now a backwater route. Most Dales bridges were rebuilt in stone in the fifty years after 1600, but were then narrow and rather humped. Grassington's bridge over the Wharfe was built in 1603, widened in 1780, regraded in 1825 and widened again in 1984. This pattern of subsequent widening was very common, and a look under almost any bridge in the national park will reveal two patterns of stonework identifying parallel arches of different ages.

Packhorse traffic created some of its own routes when it developed as a commercial freight service. No respecters of gradient, they took bold lines high over the fells and have left us with some splendid green tracks. The Craven Way climbed out of Dentdale, to a high-level route over the bleak northern slopes of Whernside, before linking the lovely line of farms down to Ellerbeck. As Kirkby Gate it traversed the length of Scales Moor, and thence to Ingleton, and the whole route remains as a right of way. Long Lane is part of the route across Ingleborough from Clapham to Selside, and Morphet Gate climbs out of West Burton on to the Wensleydale scars for a direct line to Middleham.

Tan Hill was a nucleus of the packhorse trade, and

The high arch of Ivelet Bridge across the River Swale is perhaps the most elegant in the Dales; built in 1695 for packhorses, it now safely carries cars but it is too narrow for heavy traffic.

inns were sited at a major crossroads, on the windswept fells. One inn survives, and from it four public paths radiate. All were packhorse routes, along with the Kirkby Road, though the other two roads are recent variations.

Most ancient tracks linked settlements, but there were exceptions. Mineral roads originated high on the fells, and we will return to the mines and their infrastructure later. And the drove roads positively avoided many villages. These were routes for Scottish cattle being driven south before the advent of the railway, and they kept largely to open land away from any tempting crops. The major route in from the north was up the Eden valley, taking the High Way up the east side of Mallerstang, over the Hell Gill Bridge and past the stablings of Shaw Paddock and High Dyke. Along the drove routes, markets grew to trade and regroup the stock. Gearstones was the major centre on the western route, with a weekly market till 1870, though its inn is now demoted to an outdoor hostel. The eastern routes linked markets at Askrigg, Hawes, Appletreewick and Skipton, and also the largest of all on Malham Moor. Great Close, as it is still known, often held 5,000 head of Scottish cattle while traders bargained on the sidelines.

Increasing numbers of carts, waggons and coaches demanded better road surfaces and easier gradients. In response came the turnpikes, toll roads designed for wheeled traffic, and which were better maintained and incorporated new or widened bridges. The main turnpike within the national park was from Richmond to Lancaster, authorized by Parliament in 1751. It provided a major route through Wensleydale and then followed the Roman road from Bainbridge to Ingleton. Perhaps more important was the 1795 deviation which took an easier route up Widdale; this at last put Hawes on the map, since when the town has continued to grow at the expense of the others in the dale. Nearly all the turnpikes have developed into the main roads of today, but the Old Road between Clapham and Ingleton remains in more of its original state since the 1823 diversion took the main road across Newby Moor.

By steady improvement and with only some short lengths of new route, the modern road system has grown from the turnpikes and better tracks. The relentless sweep of tarmac is often seen as a threat, especially where pleasant green tracks are lost to noisy traffic. In 1953 the road from Kettlewell over

into Coverdale was the last to be tarred in the national park, but has since remained quiet. Soon after then, there was major controversy over plans to tar Mastiles Lane as a link from Malham to Wharfedale. This would have created a busy tourist loop with no real benefit, and plans were dropped under the weight of conservationist pressure. With today's more enlightened environmental attitudes, additions or significant changes to the Dales road system should be minimal.

Large trucks laden with quarry aggregate are a conspicuous and unwelcome traffic on three park roads – Kilnsey to Skipton, Horton to Settle and for a short way down through Ingleton. It is significant that railways do follow the two longer routes, and maturing environmental values could therefore rid the park of most of this unnecessary road traffic.

Tourist traffic is very different as it is an unavoidable consequence of a popular and successful national park, and it parallels a significant decline in the rural bus services. Some roads, notably to Malham and up Wharfedale, approach saturation on hot summer Sundays, but any natural limit imposed by the roads is beneficial to the conservation of the sites and villages they feed. Large village car parks are now a necessity rather

When the stone walls were built along the route from Wharfedale over into Coverdale, they were far enough apart for a flock of sheep to be driven between them, but the modern tar is much narrower.

than a luxury. Tourist pressures will continue to increase, and car-parking provision and subtle road improvements are growing factors in the natural conflict between visitor services and conservation.

While the paths, tracks and roads of the Dales have spread through two thousand years of history, the railways occupy only a brief interlude and number but few. Any mention of railways and the Dales brings reference to the Settle to Carlisle – the boldest main-line railway in Britain, with its finest section within the national park. This railway is unusual in that it never intrudes into the park landscape; instead it is a welcome addition to the drama of the high fells.

The Settle–Carlisle is the line no one wanted. The Midland Railway only built it out of desperation to achieve a route to Scotland clear of their rivals on either coast. Opened in 1876, it was Britain's last main line. The terrain meant that it was an expensive venture, but the Midland took the challenge head-on, and ended up creating a superb monument to Victorian engineering. Thousands of men built high embankments, deep cuttings, long tunnels, and, finest of all, the great viaducts.

At Ribblehead the sweeping line of the famous viaduct is now an essential element of the Three Peaks landscape. Its twenty-four high arches are built of local limestone, hewn in blocks of up to eight tons from trackside quarries at the foot of Whernside. Now they spring from Batty Moss, a soggy peat bog twenty-five feet deep which was just one of the engineers' headaches. Further north, beyond the blackness of Blea Moor Tunnel, the railway takes a dramatic line round the upper end of Dentdale. Two more high viaducts are proud steps in the march across the highest and bleakest of the fells.

Beside the viaducts, a host of bridges and fine station buildings in local style all contribute to the environment along the line. But though the Settle–Carlisle was an engineering achievement, and a vital main line in the years of railway prosperity, its future was in doubt as the railways went into decline. In 1970 it lost its local services, though the line survived the Beeching axe as a strategic alternative to the Shap route.

In 1975, Dales Rail was instigated by the national park, and has brought local trains back to the line. Village stations have been reopened, and services are now firmly established on certain summer weekends. Feeding from Leeds, Preston and

A footpath heads clean through a wall near Muker, but the two stone uprights are close enough to allow only people, and not sheep, to pass.

A steam-hauled excursion train clears the Ribblehead Viaduct on its way north over the magnificent Settle to Carlisle railway line.

Carlisle, trains are specifically designed for ramblers and park visitors tired of congested roads, and also provide a valuable service for many local people. With linking buses and co-ordinated guided walks, Dales Rail proved welcome and a success, and in 1986 grew into a new daily service of local trains between Skipton and Carlisle. Also, since 1980, steam trains have returned to the Settle–Carlisle in another popular move.

Dales Rail and steam can finance certain trains, but track maintenance is another issue. British Rail holds no love for such an expensive line; in 1982 they ran down services to kill all demand, and the following November served notice of closure. But unprecedented public opposition has now thrust any possible closure into the political arena. If Ribblehead Viaduct is the highlight of the Settle–Carlisle, it may also be its downfall. The location is famed for its weather – a blend of wind, rain and cold as harsh as any in the Pennine winter. The notorious wind has robbed a few goods trains of their loads, and blown a number of cars off a passing train in 1964. But it is the cold that has fractured the stone, and the rain that has rotted the mortar, and the engineering strength of the viaduct is now in question.

The railway boom around 1850 saw grandiose plans for a host of lines through the Yorkshire Dales. Principal ones were those for lines up Wharfedale, and detailed plans were laid for tunnels to Coverdale, Bishopdale and Raydale. Wensleydale schemes were numerous, and included plans for tunnels to Swaledale, but reality levelled the fervour. It was 1878 before the railway linked Leyburn to Garsdale, on the Settle–Carlisle, and Hawes reaped the prosperity of the increased trade. But regular passenger services, and freight trains loaded with livestock, wool, milk and local stone could not last. Passenger trains in Wensleydale ceased in 1954, freight ended a decade later, and the tracks within the park were removed in 1965. The Hawes station buildings are now a National Park Centre.

Transport is one of the fastest developing aspects of any society, and it has come close to full circle within the national park. Railways have come, and nearly all gone. Roads have come, and are here to stay though with little prospect of future growth. Hill tracks thrived, then survived as green tracks, and the footpaths which started it all are now given a new lease of life as leisure walking grows.

7 Mine and quarry

Strong old rocks tend to have two characteristics: they form dramatic uplands suitable for national parks, and they are the ground most likely to contain minerals of economic value. It is therefore a geological fact that national parks are prime sites for mines and quarries. The Yorkshire Dales is no exception – the limestones and grits are valuable construction stones and are also host to metal ores. The rocks and minerals have clearly been a major influence in the past development of the Dales, but purely in the context of the national park they are both benefit and threat. Relics of a long history of metal mining and small-scale quarrying add a fascinating aspect to the park environment. On the

An adit entrance leads to old underground mineworkings, while old surface diggings mark the line of the lead vein up the hillside above. Waste heaps fill the foreground valley, and the skyline has the remains of the peat store for the Old Gang Smelt Mill in the Swaledale mining field.

other hand, modern large stone quarries have few redeeming qualities, and are in direct conflict with the aims of the park. Past and present have few comparisons.

For over a thousand years, Arkengarthdale was heartland to a thriving lead-mining industry. The lead mostly occurs in veins – bedrock fissures filled with various minerals, including the shiny grey

Mines and quarries.

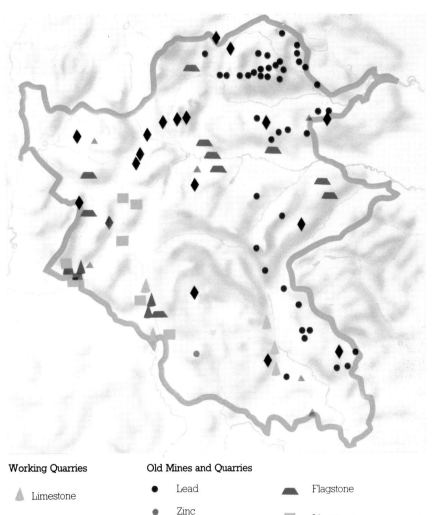

Working Quarries

🔺 Limestone

🔺 Greywacke

Old Mines and Quarries

● Lead

● Zinc

♦ Coal

▲ Grit

◣ Flagstone

■ Limestone

◣ Slate

galena which is lead sulphide. All the vein minerals were deposited over 100 million years ago by warm saline waters migrating along the fissures, and these brought the metals in solution from deep sedimentary basins to the east.

The veins vary in width. Some are only inches wide and are of no economic value, but many are five feet wide, and locally up to ten feet. When wide enough and rich enough to be mined they are known as orebodies. The patterns of bedrock and fracture movements created what the miners knew as ore shoots – areas of thick vein maybe half a mile long and over 100 feet deep.

Successful mining was finding good ore shoots. The first miners found some exposed on the surface, but others were revealed by washing the soil away or driving tunnels to intersect known veins at depth. The veins were first worked by surface digging, and then via small shafts, but larger-scale mining had to get organized, and had a choice of methods.

A feature of the Arkengarthdale orefield was the use of hushes. The miners ponded streams high on the fells, and then released a temporary torrent of water down the line of the vein. Loose rock and mineral was washed down the hillside to a prepared flatter area where the heavy lead mineral was deposited and the lighter waste rock was swept on into the river channels. While the hilltop ponds refilled, miners broke loose more of the vein material, and then repeated the process. The hushes ended up fifty feet deep and twice as wide, many reaching half a mile down the fell.

Deeper ore shoots were mined underground. Reached by either shafts from the moor tops, or

It looks like a rather straight, rocky valley, but this is the Turf Moor Hush, down a lead vein in Arkengarthdale. It was cut by the miners breaking the rock and then washing it all out with a diverted stream off the fell.

The well-preserved flue above the Cupola Mill on Grassington Moor. The smelt mill closed in 1885, but the flue-top chimney was restored in 1966.

adits, or levels, from the valley sides, workings often reached a couple of miles along a vein at depths maybe a thousand feet below the surface. The rich shoots were progressively dug out leaving large open stopes on the veins, and the ore was carted out by pony power or maybe hauled up shafts by water power.

Once at daylight, the ore was dressed by hand jigging and washing – where water washed the light waste away from the heavy galena. Packhorses then took the ore to the smelt mills. In these, the hearths were fed with both ore and coal or peat, and kept at a high temperature by a forced draught. Within the hearth, the lead sulphide was first roasted to drive off the sulphur and create lead oxide, and this was then reduced by the hot charcoal; molten lead would be tapped off the bottom of the hearth and fed into pig moulds. Nearly a ton of lead was produced in an eight-hour shift, using half a ton of coal.

The final stage of the lead process was in the flag-lined flues which led from the mills for hundreds of yards up the hillsides. These cooled the hearth gases, and lead condensed out in the soot, to be periodically scraped and washed out; about five per cent of the total lead yield was normally won from the flues.

Largest of the mining fields was Swaledale, which yielded about half a million tons of lead. Its heyday built up from 1720, but after 1840 it went into decline as the price of lead fell and fell. More than any other, this field was worked by the big hushes, which still scar the Arkengarthdale hillsides in particular. Turf Moor Hush is a fine roadside example west of Langthwaite, and the extensive Hungry Hushes lie just to its north. The hushes are numerous because most ore shoots were at high level, and for the same reason most of Swaledale's underground mining was reached by adits driven into the hillsides. Many of their stone arch entrances are still to be seen, usually with the mine drainage flowing out. At the Stone's Level, in Little Punchard Gill, the drainage fed a canal in the adit, and the ore was brought out on barges. But most adits had rail tracks, and the Faggergill Mines, which kept going till 1913, had over twenty-five miles of underground railway.

Gunnerside Gill had an important group of mines on the main belt of veins. The Sir Francis Level was started in 1864 and was the last major new project in Swaledale. It cut to a number of veins, and ore from them was taken underground through more levels to Hard Level Gill and thence to the Old Gang Smelt

Mill. This worked until 1900, and the main mill building partly survives today. The old hearth is recognizable, and the flue can be seen arrow-straight up the hillside. Standing on the hill, overlooking the valley tip-heaps, are the remains of the huge peat store which held a year's supply of fuel for the hungry hearth.

Perhaps a quarter of a million tons of lead was produced from the part of the Grassington mining field inside the national park; more came from Greenhow Hill just outside. In contrast to the adit

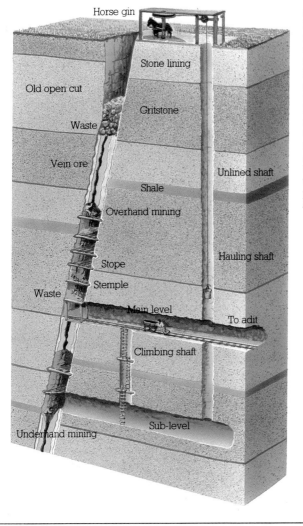

Horse gin
Stone lining
Old open cut
Gritstone
Waste
Vein ore
Unlined shaft
Shale
Overhand mining
Hauling shaft
Stope
Stemple
Waste
Main level
To adit
Climbing shaft
Sub-level
Underhand mining

Cut-away diagram of a lead vein working. The mineral occurs in a single vein, formed on a fault in the bedrock, and has been worked from the surface, but is here mined underground at two levels. Access is via an adit, with small railway tracks, and by shafts either fitted with ladders or left clear for hauling. Within the vein, timbering is used for platforms for both access and storing waste.

Remains of the Old Gang Smelt Mill, just north of Swaledale; these are now kept in good repair by the National Park under a new form of guardianship agreement.

and hush mining of Swaledale, Grassington Moor is peppered with old mine shafts, most about five feet in diameter and 400 feet deep.

In later years, the Grassington mines were well organized by the Duke of Devonshire, with the benefit of his Derbyshire experience. The Duke's Level, driven in 1790 from Hebden Beck, linked many of the mines to drain them without the cost of pumping up the shafts. Surface water was also controlled, with leat canals feeding each mine to allow ore dressing. The water came from a reservoir now known as Priest's Tarn.

This southern ore field had a more varied mineralogy than Swaledale. Silver was a major by-product in the latter years at the Cupola Mill; it occurs as a trace in some of the galena. Further west around Malham, there was little lead, but some copper ore was mined, and a bonanza discovery worked around 1800 was over 5,000 tons of calamine, zinc carbonate, filling an ancient cave passage in Pikedaw Hill. In recent years both barite and fluorspar have been worked as small ventures in the field – the last fluorspar mine was in Troller's Gill; perhaps sadly, it was the end of an era. Prospects for future mining are thin indeed.

Local coal resources were always in demand before the railways brought cheap supplies from the main coalfields. Within the national park there are thin seams in the Yoredale rocks, and numerous small mines trace the outcrops over the high fells. The old workings can be recognized by the little tip heaps of black shale, often grassed over but quite distinct from the limestone and grit waste from the lead mines. Adits and drift mines followed the seams in from the outcrops, but many workings were in bell pits. Shafts were sunk maybe fifty feet to a seam which was worked outwards until it was unsafe, and a new bell pit was then begun a few yards away. Preston Moor has over a hundred bell pits astride the park boundary between Wensleydale and Swaledale; they were worked from 1720 to 1880 to feed three nearby smelt mills. More coal pits on the summit of Fountains Fell supplied coal to lime kilns and also met domestic demand from the better seam.

The oldest coal mines in the park date from before 1300 at Tan Hill. The main seam there is four feet thick, and was worked in the last century with many miles of room and pillar workings on a grid system.

Another valuable fuel resource in the Yorkshire Dales was peat. The lead smelters consumed huge quantities which were cut from the blanket deposits on the high grit fells not far above the lead veins. Many villagers also had rights of turbary, which allowed them to cut peat for their own use from common lands on the fell. Peat cutting has now almost ceased in the national park, but old diggings can be recognized, and many more have flooded to create small tarns.

Unused flags stacked outside an abandoned flagstone mine near Carperby in Wensleydale. The flagstone bed can be seen at the mine entrance, and a limestone scar is only a little further up the hillside.

In the past, when transport was limited, almost any strong local stone was worked for building material. Small hand-worked quarries are scattered all over the Yorkshire Dales. Today they are weathered and revegetated, and many are confused with natural scars, though a common giveaway is the level terrace left on the waste material. The national park area was best known for its abundance of flagstone, the strong, thin-bedded sandstone found mainly in the Yoredale rocks. Thicker flags were used for paving and flooring, and the thinner were valued for roofing.

The southern dales lack the good Yoredale flags but have their own roofing stones. Ingleton was known for its green slates, worked from the glens. Most of the streamside quarries have now mellowed into coves, and quarries are far from the mind of many visitors to the intervening waterfalls. Also in these older rocks beneath the limestone is the flagstone quarried at Helwith Bridge in Ribblesdale, where the thicker blocks are conspicuous in most local buildings.

Massively bedded sandstone, also known as gritstone, was worked from both the Yoredale and Millstone Grit sequences. It was in demand for lintels, mullions and quoins to finish most buildings, and the best was exploited for the whole of many more elaborate Georgian houses. The Greets quarry high on the moor above Castle Bolton, yielded an excellent stone from the Yoredale Ten Fathom Grit.

Almost any of the Carboniferous Limestones could be used for rough building, walling or lime burning. All three were in active demand in the past. No dale is without limestone, and there are hundreds of little old quarries. Always the easiest source was used, and for many villagers this was the nearest scar, many of which now owe their steep profile to man's handiwork. Few limestones were anything special, though Dentdale had an attractive stone containing large crinoid fossils. It could take a polish, so was known as a marble, and the black and white varieties were highly prized, until the industry virtually died before 1900 in the face of Italian competition.

Within the national park there are about 600 abandoned lime kilns, whose stone arches adorn many an open hillside. They largely date from the eighteenth century, and produced lime to sweeten the fields, with a lesser amount for mortar. Limestone came from adjacent diggings, and coal or peat was brought from the higher fells. Layers of limestone and fuel were fed in at the top for a long, slow burn, and at night they glowed red through their porous walls. The lime was progressively drawn off through the bottom archway.

A special demand on the limestone is for smoothed and rounded stone for ornamental use on garden walls and rockeries. The material taken is just the top layer of water-fretted limestone pavements, and the workings are therefore enormously destructive, leaving behind a surface of angular unweathered rock. Through the last 100 years close on a million tons may have been removed from the limestone pavements of Ingleborough. Recent protective legislation has almost halted the damage, but a number of the park pavements have already lost their loose stone at the expense of rather tasteless wall design now adorning many villages.

Limestone is the one rock in the Yorkshire Dales which has bridged the gap to be quarried in both past and present. The sad contrast through time is

The intact stonework of an old lime kiln stands forgotten beside a small beck in Wensleydale.

provided by the modern ethic of quarry economics that big is beautiful, even though the same does not apply in an environmental context. The Carboniferous Limestone is hugely in demand as a crushed rock aggregate for use in concrete and roadstone, and less so as a chemical resource. There are five working limestone quarries within the national park, all in the lower reaches of Wharfedale and Ribblesdale. In total they produce over two million tons of stone each year, but the sad truth is that over eighty per cent of this is just for low-value aggregate for which there are abundant alternative sources.

The second group of large quarries in the park includes those in the greywacke which underlies the limestone. In the trade this rock is known as gritstone, but it is very different from the building stones of the Millstone Grit; it is a strong, compact rock which makes an excellent skid-resistant roadstone. There are two quarries just west of Helwith Bridge, with another at Skirwith above Ingleton. And further up Chapel-le-Dale, the

The giant Beecroft Quarry bites into the limestone of Ingleborough and creates a massive scar looming over the village of Horton in Ribblesdale.

Ingleton Granite Quarry, presently inactive, is incorrectly named as its stone is just a coarse grained variety of greywacke.

Eight large active quarries are more than a national park should have to'bear. The problem is that the quarries usually have valid planning permission inherited from earlier days when the environment received scant regard. Permissions cover the working quarries and three currently inactive sites around Ingleborough. Reserves covered by permissions vary between the sites, but most can cover working well into the next century.

Since new legislation in 1981, existing quarry permissions can be revoked, so the problem in the park is not as intractable as it once was. However, compensation would be an impossible financial burden unless it could be mitigated by alternative sites offered in exchange. The problem then becomes one of politics, where there is a serious lack of any national policy on quarrying in the national parks, backed by an absence of co-ordination across county planning boundaries. There is even a vital need to distinguish between demand, by the quarry companies, and need, in the national context; only the latter can be sensibly evaluated against environmental losses. Also, in the case of the Yorkshire Dales National Park, it must be recognized that the greywacke is a valuable stone with special qualities not easily matched elsewhere. On the other hand, most of the park limestone has plenty of alternatives, of both limestone and other rocks, available in less sensitive areas.

In the long term, the overriding national concern will amost certainly drift towards recognition of environmental values, and nationally based policy should enhance genuine conservation. In the meantime, the national park has to work on a smaller scale. The big quarries have to be lived with, protected by their economic weight, and, for example, the Moughton pavements are doomed to fall to the Horton Quarry. But perhaps some smaller sensitive sites can be saved, and many people would view it as a success if the Ribblehead limestone quarry was never worked again.

For the future, the quarries, as opposed to their plant and buildings, may not be the ultimate disaster. Not many passing visitors appreciate the difference between Arnberg Scar in Littondale and Stainforth Scar in Ribblesdale, but the former is the work of a glacier and part of the latter is an old quarry. A novel approach to the active quarry could turn an eyesore into a visitor attraction. In place of screening embankments, a viewing platform with information displays could make a working quarry into a feature of interest. Such action could justify a place within the national park philosophy of blending visitor amenities into a living countryside without fossilizing the resident population.

8 **Farming in the Dales**

Farming has transformed the Yorkshire Dales. It has created the landscape texture which is the essence of the national park. For more than 5,000 years man has nurtured the landscape to give it a superb balance of unique visual appeal. The haymeadows below and the moor above, the stone walls and the barns, the minimal conifer and arable cropping; the blend is just right. Within the splendid setting of the Pennine hills, the Dales farmers have made a landscape of richness and variety. The farming has never been intensive, in a style which could overrun a natural environment. The farming of the Dales has always been a low key affair – yet without it, there would be a wilderness, and a totally different kind of national park.

From the early woodland cover, man has cleared the Dales and maintained the open land by his farming. The landscape has evolved, through the generations of early clearances, the hunting forests and chases, and then the critical spread of sheep. Man has cleared the land, and also reshaped it. Most conspicuous are the medieval strip lynchets, the field terraces dating most probably from 1200–1350. A relic of the benefit of flatter land for ox-team ploughing, they were a feature of the English landscape until many were smothered by changing

A farmer uses his collie dogs to drive a flock of sheep up through the village of Conistone on to the fells above Wharfedale.

ploughing techniques. The lynchets have survived well in the pastures never attacked by the modern plough, and some of Britain's finest are now in the dales of the national park.

The medieval farming terraces known as lynchets which survive in the pasture of Littondale.

Lynchets were a component of the subsistence farming which had to dominate in medieval times. Corn was a major crop, with a mill in every dale. Even in these upland areas vegetables were grown and demanded ploughed fields. Trading and transport reduced the pressures, and the railways saw the final decline of the Dales arable land. From around 1870, sheep and cattle dominated; pasture replaced the crops, and was far more suited to the Pennine climate.

Today the land of the Yorkshire Dales falls into three categories. Valley-floor meadows are the richest farmland but form only five per cent of the national park area. Good permanent pasture spreads up the dale sides and accounts for another twenty per cent. Nearly all the rest is upland moor, wild and beautiful but only fit for grouse or limited grazing. It is a harsh distribution of land values, and it has dictated the farming practices. Nearly all Dales farms contain a mix of meadow, pasture and moor, but the proportions vary and determine the stock pattern which is applicable. One common factor is that all the land is enclosed by drystone walls.

The walls, along with field barns and the delightful vernacular architecture of the farm buildings, are among the great inheritances which characterize the national park. Thousands of miles of walls are conspicuous throughout the Dales; only in Dentdale do the skilfully laid hedges provide a common alternative. Most of the walls are between 100 and 200 years old, and were the lasting achievement of hundreds of men working over many years. A skilled man could lay about seven yards of wall a day, while others had to win the stone and carry it to the site.

The field patterns picked out by the walls belie the walls' origins. The earliest date from before

A skilled local craftsman carefully rebuilds a broken stone wall high on the limestone fell of Ingleborough.

1500, and are among the crooked irregular walls around small fields near the villages. Often built with stone cleared from the land, these were gradually extended, and in later years included the small intakes of land enclosed by the miners who farmed small plots for their own food. The enclosures of larger fields, planned by local common agreement, spread over most of the dale floors, particularly after 1750. Then came the Enclosure Acts. A classic example of power abuse by the gentry, these enabled huge takeovers of common land merely by the act of enclosing it. Largely between 1780 and 1820, most of the Dales uplands were enclosed by the long straight walls which sweep up the valley sides and right over the fells. An impressive characteristic of the national park today, the enclosure walls were a tragedy for the small farmer who lost his access to so much upland grazing.

In the meadows of the dales floor, the old stone field barns, or out barns, are as distinctive as the walls. Swaledale has a barn in nearly every field; there are sixty within half a mile of Muker. The barns were built as byres, to winter usually four cows with their feed hay kept in a loft. Siting the barns in the meadows cut the distance to carry both the hay and the manure which was returned to the field.

Sadly, the modern practice of wintering the cattle in centralized housing on the farmstead means that many redundant barns are falling derelict. Similarly, walls are left to decay where fields are too small, and the steady loss of barns and walls is a loss to the national park, though some grants can now be directed to arrest the decline. As old buildings go, new ones come, and the modern rash of huge farm sheds has created unwelcome blotches in an established landscape.

Dales farming is limited by the poor agricultural qualities of the land. Grade three land, of minimal arable value, is limited to the lower end of a few dales. Most of the dale floors are of grade four, suitable only for haymeadow or permanent pasture.

The haymeadows are not only the farmers' valued source of winter feed, but are also a treasure of the national park. A rich mixture of grasses along with innumerable wild flowers, the herb-rich meadows are especially precious, and the Swaledale landscape of haymeadows, walls and field barns is of the very highest conservation value. For most of the time the meadows are a mat of green, and the

Long evening shadows highlight the white limestone used to build the walls and field barns, here on the floor of Wharfedale just below Grass Wood. These field patterns give a distinctive texture to the finest of the Dales landscapes.

vivid colours of the flowers are only seen for a few weeks each year; late June in Swaledale is beautiful. But the haymeadows only survive with traditional farming methods, and modern intensive practices eliminate the flowers in favour of the grasses. The upland herb meadows within the national park are Britain's finest, and may rate as one of the nation's most threatened habitats.

Traditional meadow management has them grazed by sheep and cattle through much of spring. After the lambing, all stock is turned out to graze the first growth on the higher fells, and the meadow grasses and herbs are left to grow. There is almost no forced growth through fertilizers, and only the lightest of manuring and a little lime is applied. Full time is allowed for flowering and seeding, and the hay is cut in July or August depending on weather and altitude. Afterwards, the stock briefly returns to graze the 'fog' of late-season re-growth.

This conservative meadow working with only a single cut of hay yields about one and a half tons of hay per acre. With no more good land available, the farmer wishing to increase his stock faces the problem of feed for the long winter; he must either buy in hay, or increase his meadow yield. A doubling of the yield may be attained with fertilizers, but therein lies the ecological threat. Fertilizers, herbicides, heavier manuring, reseeding and land drainage can all increase yields, but they favour the grasses and reduce the floristic value and richness of the meadow. Silage – the fermented, self-pickled grass used for animal feed – can be cut twice a year from forced growths of young, wet grass; but this interrupts the herb

Harvesting the hay from a panorama of buttercup meadows in Swaledale.

Cattle returning from the milking sheds to the pastures of Swaledale above Gunnerside.

seeding and so only the grasses thrive. Also, as a result of intensification many former meadows, which were scythed by hand on slopes too steep for machinery, have reverted to grazed pasture. Quite simply, modern farming economics and environmental conservation are in conflict, through no fault of either.

Typical statistics for the three main types of farm in the Yorkshire Dales

		Area in acres		Stock numbers		
	Position	Pasture	Moor	Cattle	Sheep	Milk sales
DAIRY	Lower dale	140	0	100	0	Main income
MIXED	Mid-dale	150	150	60	300	Low yield
HILL	Upper dale	75	1,200	20	700	None

Though sheep typify the farming in the Yorkshire Dales, it is the cattle which provide the contrasts between farms. Dairy herds are only kept on the richer pasture in the lowest reaches of the dales. Nearly all milking is by machine, and daily collections by bulk tanker take the milk to town bottling plants or to creameries for cheese and butter production. Farms in the mid-dales achieve lower milk yields, reflecting the poorer pasture, and are also limited in field usability by how far the milking cow can walk back to the farm twice daily.

The wide low floor of Wensleydale has always made it a leader in Dales dairy farming. Back before 1700 there was a daily shipment of butter and cheese from Wensleydale to Yarm, and then by boat to the insatiable London markets. From 1870 there were daily milk trains on the new railway, and since about 1920 the milk output has stayed ahead of cheese. Wensleydale has long been famous for its own distinctive brand of cheese. This was originally made from ewes' milk, though the cow had taken over early in the last century. Then all the cheeses were made on the farm, just when the cows were in the pasture through the summer. In 1897 the first cheese factory opened in Hawes, and farm cheese production has been almost non-existent since 1955.

In the upper dales, store cattle replace the dairy herds. These are beasts, destined for the butcher, who are in their early growing stage before going for a final fattening. Their numbers have increased over recent decades, and though once mainly Shorthorns they are now strongly influenced by the introduction of Friesian bulls. Other than those kept to replenish the herd, they are normally sold at between six months and a year, together with the bull calves from the dairy herds; they leave the Dales, and are fattened on lowland farms.

Wintering the cattle is the critical factor in farm capacity. Within the national park, many cows are indoors from October to May, when a single beast may eat four tons of feed – or the yield of over two acres of unfertilized meadow. The field barns wintered the cattle in the past, but they are now neglected as the modern trend is to house them on the main farm unit, even though this is only essential for milking cows. Beef cattle lack the economic benefits of dairy herds, and the wintering is costly, so grant support is necessary to maintain the stocking of the upper dales farm. Store cattle with no milk sales therefore receive the Hill Livestock Compensatory Allowance, and this is an economic factor which links them to sheep.

Hill farming is sheep farming. The Yorkshire Dales offers no exception, and their whole landscape would be different without the grazing sheep. Even the national park emblem is a Swaledale tup, or ram. This is one of the black-faced breeds which dominates in the northern dales, only little different from the Dales bred which has two white patches on the face and is commoner in the southern dales. The Rough Fell, of the Howgill Hills, has irregular facial colouring, and all three breeds have splendid horns on both tups and ewes. These are moorland sheep with long wool coats, which sadly are of poor quality best fit for carpets; the main value of the wool is to the sheep itself. Pennine winters are hard and only the well-adapted breeds

A line of hungry sheep head for the banks of the Wharfe hoping to find a little grass not buried under the blanket of snow.

survive. The superb wool coats have kept sheep alive for many days buried under snowdrifts. Indeed, the main problem of snow is not the cold but its blanketing of the vegetation, and that is when the farmer may have to bring the flock off the fell and supply feed from store.

While winter is hard, lambing creates the busy season, usually in April. It is the only time when the ewes are long off the moors. The calendar follows through with shearing in early summer, followed by dipping a month later. Then in November the tups are put to the ewes. Alternatively the autumn sales see sheep off to the lowlands. Young 'gimmer' ewes are mainly kept to replenish the stock, but there are sales to lowland farmers who prefer to breed from strong hill ewes. Male 'wether' lambs are sold on for fattening, and many four-year-old ewes are also sold to the lowlands.

These market sales are a limited source of income, and only the very largest farms could survive on them alone. Hill farming, in the Dales and elsewhere, would die without great support. The aim of the Hill Livestock Compensatory Allowances is to ensure summer hill grazing by increasing the farms' wintering capacity in terms of expensive

Either traditional hand shears or modern electric clippers are used to clip the thick fleece of the Dales sheep.

feed supplies, though a problem now is that much of the fells are over-grazed. The hill farming is essential, not for the produce which is now in national surplus, but to maintain the environment for both the local population and the visitors. Loss of the sheep would let the fells and dales revert to scrub vegetation. Sheep eat out young shrubs and bushes, and it is the grasses which thrive on continued grazing. The wide fells and the bare limestone pavements owe their open aspect to the sheep, and many park visitors find this one of the attractions of the Dales landscape.

The sheep live most of the year on the fells, grazing alone or with their lambs. Even though not in flocks, most sheep are heafed. This means that they have an inherent sense of place, also passed on to their lambs, and they will seldom stray from their own patch. On unenclosed moor this is a valuable asset, saving on shepherding and also reducing spread of disease. Most sheep are on common land, which farmers have access to by owning a given number of gaits. A gait permits a farmer to graze one sheep and its lambs, and is registered with the local common-land management committee, which, if it is working well, controls the grazing to maximize regeneration of the vegetation. With upland commons forming over a quarter of the national park, these committees play a vital role in conserving the landscape. Under-grazing leads to a clogged tangle of dead herbage, while over-grazing kills the heather, just leaves the grass and encourages the growth of thistles.

The park fell land can offer alternatives to sheep farming. Grouse breeding creates lucrative shooting rights, and the heather moors of the Pennines are among England's finest. Adjacent to Wharfedale, the Conistone and Barden Moors are managed primarily for game, and grouse are an increasing influence on the fells of Swaledale.

The third use for the high fells is forestry, and this has minimal environmental benefits. The Pennine uplands are best suited for fast-growing conifers, and the planted forests are mostly Sitka spruce, with lesser amounts of lodgepole pine and larch. A sixty-year growth cycle makes extensive forestry irrelevant to the small farmer, but the tax structure makes it attractive for large absentee investors. Conifer forest now covers nearly two per cent of the national park, and most has been planted on private land in the last twenty years. Huge blocks of single-species forest are unwelcome because they smother the environment.

Without the large estates' options of grouse or forestry, the traditional Yorkshire Dales farmer still relies on sheep and cattle; first and foremost he is a superb stockman. Most farms units are small, rarely employing more than one family, and are normally owner-occupied, though this is less so in Swaledale. Life for the Dales farmer has always involved hard work. In the past, the hay was scythed by hand and then taken in on horse-drawn sleds; peat cutting was the first job after lambing, and then bracken was harvested for barn bedding. Some tasks have gone, and others have been mechanized. The Land Rover is now ubiquitous, and trail bikes and buggy trikes are used on the farm for work, not pleasure. A job which cannot be mechanized is walling, and some farms have twenty miles of drystone wall to maintain; all too often recourse has to be made to wire fencing across a collapsed section of wall. But one permanent feature of the Dales farm is the sheep dog; hill farming would be next to impossible without those superb Border collies.

Farming may be attractive in the summer, but is harsh through the Pennine winter. That's when the outlying farms are most lonely. Cosh is a long way from anywhere at the head of Littondale, and others like Gill House high on Conistone Moor are too isolated and are now abandoned. Heavy snow can incur serious sheep losses, and a bad winter can overcome the fragile economy of a hill farm. Capital costs may be low but so is income, and few hill farmers have scope for change. A breeding ewe is two years old before it yields any income beyond one meagre coat of wool. The support by grants –

Huge areas of fell can support only small numbers of grazing sheep, but these are the mainstay of the upland farms.

for building, maintenance, and hill stock – is vital to the continued farming of the Yorkshire Dales.

Numbers of both farms and farmers are on the decline in the Yorkshire Dales. Yet farming is vital to the environment, and the National Park does recognize the agricultural role in conserving the visual qualities of the landscape. The Park policy is to retain traditional practices, and to reverse the trends of farm abandonment and piecemeal wall and barn dereliction. Pasture and meadow revert to moor or scrub if left unworked, and the top end of Swaledale is currently under the greatest threat from abandonment; it has already happened higher up, in much of Birkdale. To stem the tide, one recourse is modernization, and this is frequently favoured by the new generation of progressive farmers' sons. But it too is a threat to the national park. Intensive farming, heavier fertilization and forced crops can only damage the Dales landscape. New experiments with wintering sheep in polythene housing, and two intensive pig units in Wensleydale, are among the signs of change.

The alternative to destructive decline or destructive change is to pay for conservation. Particularly in the national park, the recreational

Harvest of the hay in Wharfedale. To the farmer it may just be another job, but the result is a work of art.

and environmental value of the land must be assessed alongside its agricultural value. With the widespread current food surpluses, the pressure is off maximizing agricultural yields – the Yorkshire Dales may have more to offer the nation and its people as a national park than in terms of market produce. This does not mean ignoring the farming community; it specifically means maintaining it, in an appropriate style, with government funding, free from economic pressures which ignore the wider environment.

Hill farm subsidies already do this to some extent, but a major innovation is the establishment of Environmentally Sensitive Areas (ESAs), in a scheme launched in 1986. An ESA is defined as having ecological and landscape value, and being under threat from harmful agricultural changes; payment is then available to the farmers to conserve the natural habitat and scenic qualities, by using compatible farming practices while maintaining adequate income levels.

In 1986 six ESAs were established. One is known as the Pennine Dales, and over half its area lies within the national park. It is based on the enclosed land of the dale floors, excluding any moorland, and

Duerley Bottom farm in Sleddale is surrounded by its enclosed pasture but it is overlooked by the vastness of the open fell.

covers parts of Swaledale, Arkengarthdale, Dentdale, Wharfedale and Waldendale. The ESA approach offers, to date, the greatest opportunity to conserve some of the finest of the Dales farmed landscapes. Initially the scheme will offer annual grants to any farmer for his agreed voluntary co-operation. Traditional farming practices have created the landscape of the Yorkshire Dales, and their continuation is vital to the future of the national park which they have spawned.

9 **Natural history**

At first it may seem illogical that a chapter on natural history should follow one on farming. But here this is the correct sequence, because there is no doubt that in the Yorkshire Dales we are looking at a man-made environment. The variety and distribution of the flowers, trees, insects and animals in the national park are a function of man's influence over the last 2,000 years. There are inheritances from the past, and a few relics of primary woodland do survive, but the wildlife of the Dales is now adapted to co-existence with man.

This is not to say that the natural history is diminished. Because the Dales have long been the scene of low-intensity farming, there is a wealth of wildlife. The plant communities of Ingleborough and Malham Tarn are of international fame, and Swaledale is hardly of lesser merit. But sheep grazing has modified most of the land and the park holds no real wilderness.

Within the park, there is a wide range of environments, each with its own suite of plant and animal life. The contrasts largely relate to altitude and geology. The limestone has its open grassland and also the rock pavements around the southern dales, while the gritstones support the moorland above the northern dales. Lower altitudes enclose the sheltered woodland and the rich meadows, while wetland is found high and low.

The high moorland, so splendid on either flank of Swaledale, is characteristic of the grit and shale plateaux where waterlogged gley soils underlie a blanket of peat. The surface is a mosaic of heather, bilberry, sphagnum and cotton grass. Heather is dominant, but it is reduced by excessive sheep grazing at the expense of grass – completely so on the Howgill Fells. Conspicuous in summer are the white heads of the cotton grass, and both this and the purple moor grass form the tussocks which can make walking such hard work on some moors. There is also plenty of mat grass, together with heath rush on the drier ground, replaced by soft rush in wetter parts. Locally known as mosses, the areas of wet ground contain more of the bog moss,

Cotton grass on a wet moor.

Evening sun and the first touch of autumn colour are a lovely combination for a stand of broadleaf trees in a gulley in Coverdale.

Natural history and conservation in the Yorkshire Dales.

sphagnum, and this dominates in the mires where it has filled ancient tarns and left those disconcerting areas of quaking ground.

Colour on the moor is provided by the heather, and its acres of dramatic purple are most intense in August and early September. But the heather is more than colour, for it is food and shelter for a wealth of birdlife. The red grouse is the famous heather bird; there are thousands in the Yorkshire Dales, and many moors are managed for their

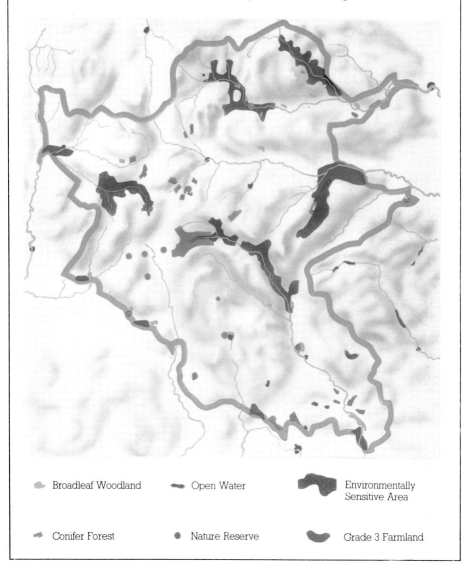

Broadleaf Woodland	Open Water	Environmentally Sensitive Area
Conifer Forest	Nature Reserve	Grade 3 Farmland

benefit. Young heather shoots are the prime food for the grouse, though the chicks also feed on insects from the sphagnum. Birds of prey such as buzzards, along with the ravens, have almost been persecuted out of the Dales, but a few merlins are making a comeback to the moors. Short-eared owls breed on the moors, and are a rare profiter from afforestation when they feed on the voles so abundant in young conifer plantations. The access land on Barden Fell is often a good place to see the moorland birds.

The long-beaked curlew, so characteristic of Swaledale.

The waders are the other major group of upland birds, nesting where they can find a large undisturbed area, and therefore lost where gripping or forestry has intruded. Swaledale is famed for its curlews, though they winter down on the coast. Oystercatchers are noisy spring visitors, and they contrast with the whistling of the golden plovers, lapwings and redshanks. Then there is the little dunlin, sometimes seen pretending to drag an injured wing to draw an intruder's attention away from a nest of chicks.

Open grassland can form on the grits but is really a feature of the limestone fells above the southern dales. The short springy turf covers a thin soil which is leached, and generally lime-deficient and acidic due to the heavy rainfall draining through it. Blue moor grass, with its tiny purple flowers in April, and the nutritious sheep's fescue are the dominant grasses, but there are many more in the upland sward.

More than any other environment, the grassland is the product of sheep grazing, left devoid of shrubs and trees as only the grasses which grow from their base can survive the constant nibbling. There is little room for other animals, though some moorland birds spread on to the grass where they can find shelter. Rabbits however are prolific, especially where a sandy soil is ideal for their burrows; but to the farmer they are a pest, as six rabbits will eat the grass that could feed another sheep. Compensation for the lean animal life is in the flowers. Abundant on the limestone hills of Malham, the fragile harebell is perhaps the most beautiful, hanging from its tall stem. Lower down in the grass is purple wild thyme, yellow rock rose and the tiny flowers of eyebright, fairy flax and salad burnet. A century ago, bunches of lady's slipper orchids were sold in Settle market, but today orchids of any type are a bit of a rarity on the Yorkshire fells.

More often the white in the limestone landscape is

A lonely hawthorn has bent to years of wind across the open limestone plateau. Now it forms a frame for a distant view of Ingleborough.

the pavement. These expanses of stark rock may seem at first to be lifeless deserts, yet they hide a fascinating botanical world. Most of Britain's finest pavements are in the national park and those of Ingleborough and Scales Moor are the most treasured. One group of primitive plants which thrive on pavement are the lichens. Sometimes orange or brown, they are usually an innocuous white and therefore easily overlooked, but lichens cover nearly all the exposed limestone; they steadily eat into the rock and largely account for the rounding of the surfaces which characterize the Dales pavements. Larger plants are mostly hidden in the grikes, those deep rock fissures which offer protection from both wind and sheep, and stay moist even through a hot summer. Grikes are harbours for the ferns and spleenworts, with perhaps the long shiny leaves of the hart's-tongue fern being the most characteristic.

An isolated tree is a dramatic intrusion on a limestone pavement. In the national park is it usually a hawthorn, except in the shelter of the sink holes and cave entrances where the rowan, or mountain ash, delights with its September crop of brilliant red berries. Trees are rare because the sheep eat out any young shoots, so the limestone pavements too are farm-modified environments. The natural conditions are only seen in some of the nature reserves, notably around the north end of Ingleborough. Scar Close has a spectacular pavement, but it is half covered in plant life – large tussocks of heather, spreading bushes of juniper and yew, and mosses in any available shade. There are the poisonous baneberry and dog's mercury,

The hart's tongue fern can often be found in the protective jaws of a grike fissure in the limestone pavements.

and then a host of colourful flowers. Trees grow undisturbed, and the nearby Colt Park has a rich ashwood, interspersed with bird cherry and rowan, all growing from very deep grikes.

On the pavements, animal life takes second place to the botany, except for the sheep, the rabbits and the occasional lizard. But where the limestone ends in scars and crags, the vertical walls are nest sites for both house martins and peregrine falcons. The magnificent peregrines are now spreading to many of the higher crags in the Dales and are among the endangered species protected within the park.

Down from the fell, the richer brown soils on the sediments of the dale floors support the luxuriant haymeadows. Natural, unfertilized meadows are becoming a rarity in Britain, and some of the finest that survive are in the Yorkshire Dales; those of Swaledale are of the very highest botanical value. The main grasses are a rich mixture of bents and fescues, with sedges and a variable content of ryegrass, cocksfoot and Yorkshire fog. But it is the flowering herbs which are so appealing and create the seas of colour each June, perhaps at their most spectacular around Muker. June is the critical time, and it is only because the single cut is traditionally left until after the herbs have seeded that the meadows can survive and not revert to pure grass. In June, Swaledale is yellow, for buttercups dominate, backed up by the splendid globe flower and the smaller meadow vetchling and birdsfoot-trefoil. Later, the meadows turn white with an adundance of pignut. Splashes of purple are provided by the lovely wood cranesbill and also by the melancholy thistle, which is not of the spiked variety, while red clover makes another contrast. Sweet cicely, more robust than its hedgerow neighbour cow parsley, adds rich cream to the palette, and springtime may yield a glory of snowdrops, especially in Littondale.

The meadow herbs attract their summer swarms of bees, and also hide a mass of smaller insect life. Butterflies are not very common, though the large heath is often seen on more open grassland. Through all the Dales fields, weasels, stoats, voles, fieldmice and hedgehogs are the usual inhabitants. Curlews and lapwings may breed in the meadows, while pied and yellow wagtails have summer nests in the stone walls. Field barns may shelter a few bats, along with house martins and swallows, but the commonest little brown bird is the meadow pipit. And the hedgerow is home for both pheasant and

Buttercups, pignut and wood cranesbill provide a feast of colour in a Swaledale meadow in June.

partridge, introduced and managed in some dales.

If moor, pavement and meadow typify the Yorkshire Dales of today, it is the woodland which can claim the historical connections. Oxenber Wood, near Austwick, may be as near as any to a primary wood; with no attempt at management, it has an open canopy of mature trees over a rich variety of undergrowth. The tough species, ash and wych elm, predominate, though the late spread of Dutch elm disease is leaving purer ashwoods for the future. There is also holly, and higher altitudes see more birch and hazel.

Ash is already dominant on the limestone, as in those straggling stands below Malham Cove, and it may be joined by some sycamore and alder. Grass Wood, in Wharfedale, is a superb spread of ash, and is a haven for birds. There are nuthatch, dunnock, blue tits and woodpeckers, as well as introduced pheasant. The leafy shade can hide the pastel-blue giant bellflower or sometimes a carpet of primrose, lily of the valley and blue moor grass. Elsewhere in the park, some fine linear woods remain uncleared along the scars of the Yoredale limestones and also up some deeper beck ravines.

There are a few places in the national park where gritstone does not just form high open moor; where the geology and shelter are right, oak is a component of the woodland. The Strid Woods, along the banks of the lower Wharfe, are splendid. It is mainly the sessile oak which grows here, distinguished by its stalkless acorns and stalked leaves in contrast to the typically lowland pedunculate oak. The trees are majestic, shrouded in golden colours through autumn and set in seas of bluebells in spring; these woods are also noted for their fungi, butterflies and birds. The Ingleton glens house fine old mixed woods, and may contain the last colony of red squirrels in the Dales. Away from the tourist trails, these and many other woods now shelter increasing numbers of deer.

The woods offer winter shelter for the animals, and sheep and rabbits far outnumber the deer. Once in the shelter, they eat the bark off the trees, especially when snow blankets the alternative ground feed; taking all the bark at head height, sheep and rabbits often ring a tree, and very effectively kill it. This is a serious problem in the Dales, and without effective fencing there is little prospect of a long-term future for much of the broad-leaved woodland. Furthermore, young shoots are completely eaten, and the trees cannot

regenerate. This is an even greater problem where the trees are coppiced. The hazels of the Freeholders' Wood, at Aysgarth Falls in Wensleydale, traditionally coppiced in early January, are now under the ownership of the National Park. The bole or stump of the tree then grows new shoots, at about three feet per year, which after seven years are strong enough to be cut and used.

Coppicing is a traditional use of the woods which does survive, but in the past there was also demand for larger timber. From around 1800, many small plantations were created, of both broad-leaved and conifer, which are now a welcome feature in the landscape texture. Sadly, new planting is rare, except for the large conifer forests which are almost devoid of any redeeming ecological value.

The important wetlands of the national park are at Malham Tarn, notable for its unusually high altitude, and the smaller one at Semer Water, besides the various mires scattered over the moors. Malham has swampy fen with sedge, brown mosses and purple moor grass, and also acidic peat bog consisting of sphagnum and cotton grass. On the drier raised bogs, moorland plants spread in, with bilberry and

Autumn colour is beautiful in the oak woods beside the River Wharfe between Bolton Priory and the Strid.

heather, and then patches of birch-wood establish. These are followed by willow and alder, to form the dense scrub known as carr. Dashes of colour are provided by the early purple of the dog violet and the lovely pink of the bird's-eye primrose, with the delicate white grass of Parnassus coming late in the summer.

All the wetland communities are complex and sensitive to change. A special variety is found in the calcareous flushes, where seepage from limestone springs nurtures rich suites of flowers and mosses. In Gordale in particular, the lime-rich waters foster the algae and moss which cause the deposition of the tufa, eventually coating and burying all the stream plant life.

Algae also floor much of Malham Tarn, that most unusual of lakes surrounded by limestone. Its water is all from springs, and this deposits lime on the tarn bed, but it still supports a host of snails and caddisflies, and some dragonflies. Perch and trout now live in the tarn, and migrating ducks seasonally gather on its waters. Semer Water is rather similar, but is known for its planktonic wealth and the mayfly population, on which feed bream, crayfish and introduced perch. It too sees migrating ducks, but the birdlife is often richer on some of the reservoirs.

The River Wharfe is a noted trout stream, but many of the Dales rivers contain roach, grayling, dace and barbel. Both rivers and becks attract the birdlife, and the agile dippers feed by hopping and diving through the cascades. Also common on the water, but not in it, are wagtails and sandpipers, and an occasional kingfisher is seen scanning the Wharfe. Sand martins feed off insects on the wing and nest in the banks of the streams. There they may be joined by a badger in the steeper, rocky gorges, along with the inevitable mink. The otter is everyone's favourite, and is known on the Bain, Ure and Wharfe; its habitat is however being lost through the steady clearance of bank vegetation.

From the grouse of the high moor to the otter of the quiet river, there is an enchanting range of wildlife in the Yorkshire Dales. But for most park visitors the animals are elusive to the eye, and perhaps their memory lies more with the plant life, whether it is buttercup meadow or heather fell.

Morning mist hangs beneath the riverside trees.

10 Recreation and leisure

There are 1,100 miles of footpaths and bridleways through the Dales, offering everything from quiet riverside strolls to bold summit traverses. The national park must come close to ideal walking country, with plenty of wild high fell but also infinite variety. A traverse between two dales can pass meadow and farmland, cross limestone pavement and peat bog, and contrast distant views with sheltered valleys.

The Dales has its share of long distance footpaths. Grandest of them all, the Pennine Way traverses the park south to north, in essence along the Pennine crest but taking in Malham Cove, Pen-y-ghent, Great Shunner Fell and upper Swaledale. Many claim that the finest section of this monumental footpath is through the Yorkshire Dales. An easier line takes the Dales Way through Wharfedale and Dentdale to provide a popular trans-Pennine walk.

A lonely walker framed by the distinctive terraced profile of Ingleborough rising from Chapel-le-Dale.

This footpath is now recognized as a recreation route, along with the Ribble Way whose upper end comes into the park.

Beside these long distance footpaths, there are other well-established routes. Most famous of all is the Three Peaks route, a classic walk linking Ingleborough, Pen-y-ghent and Whernside in a single long day. It is a challenge and an inspiration in some of the best limestone country, though its popularity is creating serious problems of footpath erosion which the National Park is attempting to

Long distance footpaths and leisure facilities.

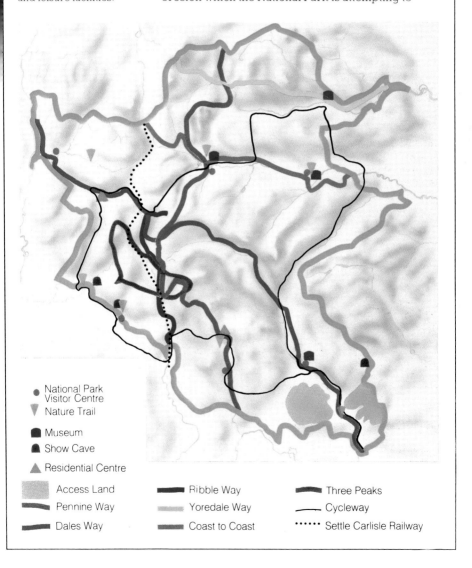

● National Park
  Visitor Centre
▼ Nature Trail
◼ Museum
◼ Show Cave
▲ Residential Centre

   Access Land
   Pennine Way
   Dales Way

   Ribble Way
   Yoredale Way
   Coast to Coast

   Three Peaks
— Cycleway
•••• Settle Carlisle Railway

solve with a major restoration project. Traversing the northern slopes of Swaledale, Wainwright's 'Coast to Coast Walk' has become a classic route linking the three parks of the Dales, the Moors and the Lakes. And the latest of the crop is the Yoredale Way along the River Ure.

The Yorkshire Dales footpaths have largely been established by long tradition, and are now public rights of way, though largely across private land. With the exception of the agreed access area on Barden Fell, there is no automatic right of access to nearly all the land in the national park. Even common land is only common to specified farms. But while the farmland of the dale floors must remain undisturbed, walkers are generally accepted over most of the high moorland. When showing reasonable concern for the environment, the walker can find many of the fells open to him with the owner's agreement, even beyond his rightful footpath.

Footpath erosion is a serious problem now being tackled by the National Park. The worst cases are on popular paths over the peat moors. Trampling soon creates a quagmire, and attempts to go round it merely widen the scar. Parts of the Three Peaks route and the Pennine Way are suffering badly, but the remedy is not simple. Stonework, boardwalk and laid chestnut palings all have their own cost and environmental problems; and the future promises more. Success has been easier on some busy lowland paths, and the newly built routes up Gordale and round Malham Cove are now widely accepted. While attempting to find new ways of managing eroded paths, the National Park is also directing the visitor away from the worst areas to allow these to recover.

Fell running is an extremely energetic sport, where the scenic benefits count for little. The Three Peaks Race is the most famous, held each April, when some runners cover the route in around three hours, and watching the race may be preferable to participation. Sadly it is another nail in the coffin of footpath erosion, especially with its early date when the ground is still wet, but some traditions are not easily changed. Village sports days are still popular in the Dales, and all-comers crag races are regular events, that at Kilnsey being one of the better known. And then there is the Fellsman Hike, a two-day event linking Ingleton and Threshfield by an arduous route over the southern summits.

The park's nature trails are designed for those

who wish to walk in pleasant surroundings. The Ingleton Waterfalls Walk is a geological classic, highlighting Thornton Force, and which also traverses splendid primary woodland and offers some fine views. There are woodland trails at Clapham, on southern Ingleborough, and by the Strid on the lower Wharfe, with the former featuring the exotic species introduced by Reginald Farrer. At Malham Tarn a boardwalk trail across the wetland is accessible by permit from the Tarn House, and there are plans for a new trail in the Freeholders' Wood at Aysgarth Falls. Much older is the trail at Hardraw Force, looping behind the waterfall and taking in a fine flagged path through the upper woods. A new type of scheme is the Sedgwick Trail, in memory of Dent's famous geologist; created in 1984 this short path traces the splendid geology where the River Clough crosses the Dent Fault near Sedbergh.

The outdoor sports draw their own enthusiasts to the national park, and caving perhaps most of all characterizes the Yorkshire Dales. Ingleton is the centre for the sport, though the caves lie right across the southern dales, from Kingsdale to Wharfedale, and beyond in both directions. They include many of the finest in Britain. Gaping Gill must be the most famous Yorkshire cave, with its miles of passages and shafts under Ingleborough reaching a depth of 665 ft (203 m), and in 1983 they were explored right through to the Ingleborough Cave resurgence. Pursuing a mixture of sport, adventure and science, the cavers can enjoy the rare opportunity to explore where man has never been before. Caves are discovered anew every year in the Dales, and it is difficult to even guess at what still remains unseen within the limestone hills.

There are three show caves within the park. White Scar Cave, near Ingleton, has a noisy, active streamway, while there are just silent old chambers in Stump Cross Cavern, east of Grassington. Ingleborough Cave, on the south side of the hill, has no road access and so is less visited, but unfairly so because it has splendid large passages and stalagmite decorations. It is also the outlet for the Gaping Gill Cave, and a winch is rigged on the famous shaft over the two summer bank holidays, so that visitors can enjoy the unforgettable descent into the main cavern. Yordas Cave, in Kingsdale, was only a show cave in Victorian times, but its chamber and waterfall can still be visited by those with boots and torches. Yordas is the rare exception to the rule

A caver abseils down a noisy waterfall in Diccan Pot, part of the Alum Pot cave system on Ingleborough.

that casual visitors should not venture underground.

The great limestone face of Malham Cove is like a magnet to rock climbers who enjoy the challenge of vertical acrobatics. Some of the established routes follow the thinnest of cracks, and nearly all provide dramatic exposure. After the cove, the walls of Gordale Scar and the great overhang of Kilnsey Crag are the most popular climbing sites, though shorter routes are made on many limestone scars.

Caves and crags may typify the Dales, but recreation spreads wider in the park. Snow in the Pennine winter is inevitable but unpredictable, and skiers therefore find no permanence, though short tows sometimes operate in Wharfedale and Dentdale. Hang-gliders come to Wharfedale and Wensleydale when the wind is right, and calmer days often see a hot-air balloon over the southern dales.

For those more attached to the ground, cycling has become very popular. The level dale floors ease the pedalling, and cycles can now be hired from some village garages. For long distance riders there is a pilot scheme for a Yorkshire Dales cycleway. This takes in the best of the landscape, both through the dales and over the fells, while

Pony trekkers take the easy way up onto the fells above Wharfedale.

An angler samples the
Ribble at Stainforth Force.

avoiding the worst of the car traffic.

The Wharfe is a renowned trout stream of the highest quality, and its fishing rights are all controlled, though some are open to rental. The other Dales rivers can also yield a catch, there is limited boat fishing by permit on Malham Tarn, and Kilnsey now has a trout farm.

Tourism, sightseeing and 'a day in the country' cover a multitude of concepts, but are all essential components of a national park. The Yorkshire Dales is a natural magnet for those wanting to enjoy the open country where there is also a touch of the unusual or spectacular. Malham is the most conspicuous attraction, and deservedly so with its dramatic limestone at both the cove and Gordale. Though the village can be swamped by people some summer Sundays, there are still times when peace reigns – even in good weather. Aysgarth Falls and Bolton Priory are the other sites which can claim popularity close to that of Malham.

For those who pursue an interest, the national park has geological, biological and archaeological delights in profusion, as the previous pages have begun to outline. But then for many visitors, the built environment is the appeal of the Yorkshire Dales.

Wharfedale may rank in front with a selection of villages, rich in the vernacular architecture, which can best be described as charming. And Dent is on its own, with its cobbled street and whitened houses. Books and television have even created new attractions: lower Wensleydale is the heart of Herriot country, and Arncliffe, in Littondale, was home to the original 'Emmerdale Farm', though it sees no filming these days.

The road right beside the Wharfe through Langstrothdale is a popular spot for motorists and summer picnickers.

Within the villages, craft workshops are a renewed trend. They are dominated by potteries, but there is the ropeworks in Hawes and a working iron forge at Thoralby. The folk museums at Hawes and Grassington give a wonderful feeling for the traditional life of the Dales, as does the museum at Reeth which also features the old mining in Swaledale. In addition, museums very relevant to the park lie just outside its boundaries at Skipton, Pateley Bridge, Settle and Richmond.

A calendar of events within the national park shows considerable variety, with something special nearly every day through the summer. The village shows with traditional items like sheep-dog trials and stone walling: Kilnsey, Malham and Reeth are just the notables, all held in August, and Tan Hill is distinguished by having a show but no village. The weekly markets: Tuesday in Hawes and Wednesday in Sedbergh. The Hardraw brass band competition in May, the Georgian days at Grassington in December, steam days on the Settle–Carlisle, the fell race days. These are but a few from a long list of events.

All this provides just a taste of the recreational opportunities in the national park. A glance through

Morning mist clinging to the floor of Wharfedale profiles the unmistakeable overhang of Kilnsey Crag.

the host of books will show that there is much more to the Yorkshire Dales, for which there cannot be space in these pages. And then there are the National Park Visitor Centres – at Aysgarth Falls, Clapham, Grassington, Hawes, Malham and Sedbergh. Not only do they supply the immediate information, but they also carry displays and exhibitions on certain themes. On a cycle of renewals and up-dates, the new addition in 1986 was at Clapham describing the caves and karst of the Dales. Each display is a fascinating insight, and it is National Park policy to ensure the visitor is well informed.

11 A challenging future for the National Park

Within the Yorkshire Dales there are the most magnificent of landscapes which attract multitudes of visitors for the purposes of tourism, recreation and environmental study. But the park also encloses a thriving community of people who live and work inside its boundaries. Predominant among these are the farmers, who, in the face of hill farming's survival only when backed by government grant support, continually strive to improve their land and its economic yield. The challenge of park management is to devise policies and programmes of work which do not just reconcile the inherent conflict between the needs of visitors, the needs of farmers and the conservation of the parks but which create a community of interest between these several needs. Support for a thriving traditional agriculture, the style which helped to create the

Wind-surfers on Semer Water.

New trees planted on Barden Fell require protective fencing to keep away the marauding sheep until they are established.

landscape of the park, will help to keep it beautiful as well as productive; and recreation and tourism create employment and sustain local services for the visitor without which the local peoples' lives would be the poorer.

The principal body charged with this balancing act in the park is the Yorkshire Dales National Park Committee. This is a component of the county council, and essentially has the powers of a planning authority. Its principal duties are twofold: to preserve and enhance the natural beauty of the area – and this includes the landscape character, the wildlife and cultural heritage; and to provide suitable opportunities for public enjoyment within the park. In addition, the National Park Authority is obliged to have due regard to the needs of agriculture and forestry and the social and economic needs of the local community.

In practice, the work is achieved by a central staff of about fifty, responsible for forward planning, development control, information and warden services, landscape conservation and recreation and access. It is fundamental that the National Park Committee has only limited powers, principally under the planning laws, and cannot either control

The traditional drystone walls collapse all too easily when walkers casually climb over them; so the installation of a timber stile makes a footpath viable without damaging the environment.

tourists or force a farmer to change his land use. They can only provide encouragement and advice and offer certain financial incentives to others to collaborate in achieving national park purposes. Yet, if tourism or any economic development was allowed to increase unchecked, we should be in danger of destroying the beauty and solitude which are the essence of the park itself. The park management can only ensure a successful future through a fair compromise under the weight of a multitude of pressures.

Conspicuous among the pressures on the park is that from the tourism and recreation. Perhaps most annoying are the cars and caravans which can sometimes choke the roads, but in addition the growing numbers of walkers make footpath erosion a major problem. It is significant that the Park Committee is not a tourist authority, and has no duty to promote tourism; yet of course, tourism can help to support the local economy and is therefore developed to a limited extent.

A prime activity within the park is therefore to increase awareness and understanding of what the park stands for and how it works. This is achieved through the Visitor Centres, Information Points in village shops, and a back-up of outdoor interpretation panels, publications and wardens' activities such as guided walks. The spread of information aims to give visitors the sense of being somewhere special, so that the park can grow from a concept to a reality, and people may ultimately appreciate the reasons for its conservation.

The future poses a picture of heavy recreational pressure on the 1100 miles of footpath in the park.

Building interior walls with breeze blocks is a major convenience and economy in new houses; but the outside walls of gritstone blocks retain the traditional character of the Dales architecture.

The erosion problem is serious and may well get worse before it is solved. The Three Peaks, the Pennine Way and perhaps a network of 'trunk-route' footpaths will need substantial construction projects, and will involve major finance. It seems that outdoor pursuits will inevitably grow, nationwide, and new facilities will no doubt be required in the Dales.

The relationship between recreation and conservation is taking a new turn. Economic pressures lead government policy to favour development of tourist infrastructure and its resultant employment potential. But the landscape is a finite resource which can be destroyed by developments for visitors. So conservation is essential if the Yorkshire Dales are to remain attractive and tourism and recreation are to continue to flourish.

A more blatant conflict with the wider national park objectives is provided by the stone quarrying in Ribblesdale and Wharfedale. Employment at the quarries makes a small but significant contribution to the economy of the Dales community, but it should not be at any cost. The environmental desecration by these quarries is disproportionate to their local economic benefits, but the legacies of past over-generous planning consents mean that the park's quarries are likely to expand still further. Even the methods of environmental assessment of quarries in force today are sadly inadequate, and the future of quarrying in the park awaits a clearly defined national policy on rock aggregate demands and resources.

National Park policy is to conserve the dales villages, but there are strict limits as to what such a

policy, or the Park budget can achieve. Currently there is the threat of losing many country bus services, which would be a major blow to the more remote villages whose social fabric is already suffering from the drift away from the countryside. Tangible successes are gained through the use of planning law to maintain or improve the environment of the villages, and conserve the buildings and the ancient monuments. Within the Yorkshire Dales there are over 600 listed buildings, whose good repair is then compulsory on the owners. Grant support is available from the National Park and from local government sources, and is therefore some positive contribution towards conservation of the cultural heritage so precious in the Dales. One scheme involves some old Swaledale smelt mills, whereby the National Park agrees with the owner to take responsibility for these fascinating old buildings. More positive action such as this will pave the way to further successes in conservation of the Dales' built heritage.

Tourism, industry, transport, buildings: they are all components of the park on which the future depends, but in the overall scheme the major concern is over the farming. This is the force which

The Pennine Dales Environmentally Sensitive Area encompasses and seeks to maintain the traditional farming landscape of hay meadows, stone walls and isolated field barns, here at its finest in the heart of Swaledale.

has created much of the character of the Dales landscapes. Farming typifies the complexity of national park issues. Farming must be in tune with conservation of landscape and wildlife if the leisure interests are to be satisfied, yet farming is under considerable pressure to change.

The farmers have been traditional stewards of the land, and are the greatest ally of the national park in

The flight of steps built up the west flank of Malham Cove is now just a thin line in the landscape, and is a vast improvement on the wide swathe of destroyed grass which was trampled in through earlier years.

the sense that they have helped create and continue to maintain the living landscape of the Dales. There is however a recurrent problem in that hill farming is only possible with artificial grant support from central government. In direct conflict with the farmers' desire for efficient modern farming, the national interest is for conservation of the landscape and its natural history and for the blending of farm activities with visitor access to the high fells. The issues could hardly be more complex. They can polarise to two extremes. One trend is towards intensive farming with higher yields, which threatens the traditional character of the Dales. The other is the maintenance of the traditional farming practices which lack economic benefit but provide the pattern, the colour, the life and the interest of the Dales landscapes. A delicate balance has to be achieved. This balance is not easily reached. Overgrazing of the higher land, with maximum stocking levels, destroys the variety of plants and herbs in favour of monotonous grass, as do improvements to the flower-rich hay meadows through the application of modern fertilizers. Drainage of the moorland by gripping with trench networks appears attractive to the farmer and is still grant-aided; yet it disrupts the moorland ecosystem and has now been shown to be ineffective as it only drains strips of land within a few feet of the actual grips. And modern farming does not need field ponds nor does it make use of the products of broad-leaved woodland; the ponds are filled and the woods are neglected, and precious wildlife habitats are lost along with their aesthetic qualities.

Up to now the Park Authority has been successful, on a limited scale, in persuading, advising and grant-aiding the farmers to keep traditional features and practices. But government has recognized the problems with, among other measures, the establishment of the Pennine Dales Environmentally Sensitive Area (ESA). This has the potential, through adequately financing traditional farming systems, to perpetuate at least some of the richness and beauty of the Dales landscape. Incentive payments are available to farmers for not introducing intensive methods which can destroy the natural ecology. In addition, sites of special scientific interest, established by the Nature Conservancy Council, impose careful restrictions on changes to the natural land and are backed by compensation agreements for loss of farming value. And nature reserves are kept as islands of species diversity, often free of sheep and carefully managed, but they can only cover tiny areas within a farmed landscape.

Until recently, farm buildings and afforestation schemes have escaped the net of normal planning legislation, and schemes beneficial to individuals have proceeded to the detriment of the broader values of the national park. Now, just within the national park, they will require the agreement of the Park Authority and the system of advice and discussion between landowners and the Park can continue backed up by the power of law where necessary. The law can play but a small part, however. Increased co-operation must be the way forward in conserving the unique values of the Yorkshire Dales.

Further beneficial policy change is seemingly inevitable. The national parks will clearly benefit from the national trend of increasing environmental awareness. But a more direct influence arises from the food surpluses now a feature of Britain, Europe and much of the world. Britain produces too much food, and patterns of farming must change. It can be claimed that one tenth of our farmed land must come out of production and be 'set aside'. The threat lies in what would happen if it was the marginal land –

A limestone pavement and the distant profile of Ingleborough provides a lingering memory of the Yorkshire Dales.

which includes most of the national parks – that was set aside, and thereby lost its vital farm management. The alternative would be for a proportion of land of all types to be set aside, with grants made to maintain traditional farming rather than intensive modern systems or for alternative crops, which are in demand, to replace those of the food mountains. Most imaginative of all would be the principle of Integrated Rural Development, combining the concept of ESAs with tourism and local industry development designed to conserve and maintain both the countryside and a thriving community.

The Yorkshire Dales could benefit from the latter alternatives, but implementation will inevitably take some years to evolve. Meanwhile, there are some specific changes needed in the park in the short term. For example, a reassessment of animal numbers on the hill land is long overdue, as current grant systems actually encourage destructive over-grazing of the heather moors,and there is a strong case for withdrawing the grants for drainage gripping. As the ESA's evolve the Swaledale and Wharfedale sites could justify extension to include the Gunnerside and Conistone reaches. Even the park itself could do well to tidy some of its ragged boundaries and expand just a little to include the northern half of the Howgills, the end of the cavernous limestone west of Kingsdale and the upper end of Nidderdale.

So the future of the national park is uncertain. It will continue to exist, but there are choices to be made concerning how positively and constructively it will mature and develop. Public opinion will count for a lot, and a growing love and respect for the countryside should promote the growth of a stronger national park system, backed up by greater financial and legislative power. The Yorkshire Dales is a splendid landscape; we have experienced it, and we must ensure it is conserved for future generations to enjoy.

Selected places of interest

ARNCLIFFE (SD 932718) Lovely village in the finest part of Littondale. Limestone houses set round an open green, and St Oswald's church in splendid setting by river.

AYSGARTH (SE 003884) Small village distant from St Andrew's, the mother church for Wensleydale. Three waterfalls down the Ure, overlooked by Freeholders' Wood and the old Yore Mill. Park Visitor Centre.

BAINBRIDGE (SD 934902) The large village green is surrounded by old houses and a restored mill, and overlooked by Roman fort site on its drumlin. Semer Water is two miles up Raydale.

BOLTON PRIORY (SE 072539) Impressive remains of the old priory overlook parkland beside the Wharfe. Beautiful mixed woods line the banks upstream to the white water of the Strid ravine.

BUCKDEN (SD 942771) Small village on a splendid site between the heights of Buckden Pike and the lovely limestone valley of Langstrothdale stretching away to the west.

BURNSALL (SE 032612) Gritstone village with old church of St Wilfrid's, on a lovely reach of the lower Wharfe accessible by riverside paths.

CLAPHAM (SD 744692) Old village with houses lined up either side of its beck. Up the stream for Clapdale Woods, the show cave, Trow Hill gorge, Gaping Gill pothole and Ingleborough summit. National Park Visitor Centre.

DENT (SD 706870) Old houses line a cobbled street in unusual style. It is the key village for Dentdale and Bartondale and has its own high altitude station on the Settle–Carlisle Railway.

GRASSINGTON (SE 003640) Lively main town in Wharfedale, with shops, inns and museum around cobbled square. Up the High Street to the grit moor and old lead mines. National Park Visitor Centre.

HAWES (SD 873898) Key town in Wensleydale, with wide High Street and important livestock market. Past the church and the older houses to reach Gayle, or across the valley to Hardraw Force. National Park Visitor Centre and adjacent museum.

HORTON (SD 808725) In the heart of Ribblesdale limestone country and in between Ingleborough and Pen-y-ghent, therefore the main centre for the Three Peaks walkers or runners. Ignore the quarry and it is an attractive village.

INGLETON (SD 695732) Lively village on the edge of the Park beneath the splendid limestone country of Chapel-le-Dale and Kingsdale. Therefore a centre for cavers, and the waterfalls and glens are equally popular with tourists and geologists.

KETTLEWELL (SD 970724) Charming village built around a beck in the finest reach of Wharfedale. Popular with visitors, hence the three inns, and overlooked by limestone scars and Great Whernside.

KILNSEY (SD 975678) Just an inn and a few houses almost beneath the dramatic limestone Crag. Now with a trout farm, and famed for its village show on August bank holiday Tuesday.

LANGTHWAITE (NZ 005025) Cramped little village in the heart of Arkengarthdale beneath fells rich in the remains of the old lead-mining industry.

MALHAM (SD 901628) Justifiably the most popular tourist centre in the Dales. Easy access to the best of limestone country with the unique Cove, the Tarn and Gordale Scar. National Park Visitor Centre.

MUKER (SD 910978) Largest of three lovely villages – the others are Thwaite and Keld – in upper Swaledale. Beautiful haymeadows on the valley floor, and splendid moors above – on Buttertubs Pass, over Great Shunner Fell or up the wilds of Birkdale.

REETH (SE 038993) Principal village of Swaledale with a long history of lead mining. Fine old houses ring the green; there is a museum and an August show.

SEDBERGH (SD 657922) Quiet market town with Norman motte-and-bailey site on Castlehaw, sixteenth-century school and seventeenth-century Quaker meeting house. Overlooked by the Howgill Fells. National Park Visitor Centre.

TAN HILL (NY 897067) No village now, just an inn, and the drama of endless grit moors. The May show is a tradition from olden times of trade and mining.

WEST BURTON (SE 016866) Splendid old village round a very large green with mill and waterfall at the bottom end. At the top there is no other road out of the secluded Walden valley.

Bibliography

Duerden, Frank *The Countryside of the Yorkshire Dales*, Jarrold, 1977.

Dunham, K C and Wilson, A A *Geology of the Northern Pennine Orefield, Volume 2, Stainmore to Craven*, British Geological Survey, HMSO, 1985.

Forder, John, Forder, Eliza and Raistrick, Arthur *Open Fell, Hidden Dale*, Frank Peters, 1985.

Harrison, Barry and Hutton, Barbara *Vernacular Houses in North Yorkshire and Cleveland*, John Donald, 1984.

Hartley, Mary and Ingibly, Joan *Life and Tradition in the Yorkshire Dales*, Dent, 1968.

Raistrick, Arthur *The Pennine Dales*, Eyre Methuen, 1968.

Raistrick, Arthur *Buildings in the Yorkshire Dales*, Dalesman, 1976.

Raistrick, Arthur *Malham and Malham Moor*, Dalesman, 1983.

Raynor, D H and Hemingway J E (editors) *The Geology and Mineral Resources of Yorkshire*, Yorkshire Geological Society, 1974.

Wainwright, A *Wainwright on the Pennine Way*, Michael Joseph, 1985.

Waltham, A C (editor) *Limestones and Caves of North-West England*, David and Charles, 1974.

Waltham, Tony *Yorkshire Dales: Limestone Country*, Constable, 1987.

Wright, Geoffrey *Roads and Trackways of the Yorkshire Dales*, Moorland, 1985.

In addition, the Yorkshire Dales National Park Initial Plan and its First Review were published by the National Park Committee in 1977 and 1984.

Most of the area of the national park is covered by the Ordnance Survey Land ranger 1:50,000 map sheet 98 and by the 1:25,000 Leisure Maps sheets 2, 10 and 30.

There are also numerous small books and leaflets on many subjects published by the National Park Authority and by Dalesman.

Useful addresses

Yorkshire Dales National Park
Colvend
Hebden Road
Grassington
Skipton
North Yorkshire BD23 5LB
(Tel: Grassington (0756) 752748)

Countryside Commission
Yorkshire and Humberside
Regional Office
8a Otley Road
Leeds LS6 2AD
(Tel: Leeds (0532) 742935)

Field Studies Council
Malham Tarn Field Centre
Malham
via Settle
North Yorkshire BD24 9PU
(Tel: Airton (07293) 331)

National Trust
Yorkshire Regional Office
27 Tadcaster Road
York YO2 2QG
(Tel: York (0904) 702021)

Nature Conservancy Council
North-East England
Regional Sub-Office
Thornborough Hall
Leyburn
North Yorkshire DL8 5AB
(Tel: Wensleydale (0969) 23447)

York Archeological Trust
1 Pavement
York YO1 2NA
(Tel: York (0904) 643211)

Yorkshire and Humberside
Tourist Board
312 Tadcaster Road
York YO2 2HF
(Tel: York (0904) 707961)

Yorkshire Dales Society
152 Main Street
Addingham
via Ilkley
West Yorkshire LS29 0LY
(Tel: Ilkley (0943) 607868)

Yorkshire Wildlife Trust
10 Toft Green
York YO1 1JT
(Tel: York (0904) 59570)

Council for National Parks
45 Shelton Street
London WC2H 9HS
(Tel: 01 240 3603)

Index